PART ONE

PRE-COMMUNIST CHINA

Let us begin with what you already know about modern China. Try doing this quiz before you read any further. Then check your answers and work out your score using the key on page 47.

Quiz

Cross out the answers you think are wrong. (NB Some questions have more than one answer.)

1 China is smaller than/about the same size as/much bigger than Europe.

2 The capital of China is Hong Kong/Tokyo/Beijing/Manila/Rangoon.

3 Most Chinese are Communists: true/false.

4 The Chinese language is understood by more people in the world than any other language: true/false.

5 Most Chinese live in communes: true/false.

6 Chinese people read and write in vertical lines from the top right hand corner to the bottom left hand corner of a page: true/false.

7 The Chinese unit of money is the Yen/Yuan/Rupee/Dong/Won.

8 The Irrawaddy/Yangzi/Yellow/Ganges are rivers in China.

9 China possesses nuclear weapons: true/false.

10 All Chinese workers are paid the same wages: true/false.

11 The most commonly drunk beverage in China is wine/vodka/tea/beer/soup.

12 The most common religion practised in China is Buddhism/Christianity/Islam/Ancestor Worship/Daoism.

13 There are fewer motor cars per head in China than in any other country in the world: true/false.

14 China has the largest army in the world: true/false.

15 The most commonly eaten foods in China are noodles/rice/cheese/fruit/poultry.

16 Chinese houses are generally made of paper and wood in case of earthquakes: true/false.

17 Hand-shaking/kissing/bowing/hugging/clapping are the two most common forms of greeting in China.

18 Chinese people invented all the following except: gunpowder/the suspension bridge/spectacles/paper money/the computer.

19 China is the world's biggest producer of all the following except: rice/cotton fabric/millet/tea/tobacco.

20 Nearly a quarter of all human beings today are Chinese: true/false.

You now know – if you didn't know it already – that nearly a quarter of all the human beings alive today are Chinese. The quiz will also have shown you that the country in which they live is very different from the English-speaking countries of the West. Yet the average quiz score shows that many of us in the West don't know very much about a quarter of the human race.

It is always easier to understand other people when you know something about their history. The aim of this book is to help develop your understanding of the Chinese people by looking at the remarkable events of the past century. We will start in the year 1900 – the Year of the Rat in the Chinese 'cycle of the years' – as China was preparing to enter the twentieth century.

1

CHINA IN 1900

The Manchu dynasty

When the Chinese study their own history, they do not refer to dates as we do in the West. They divide their history into dynasties – periods of time when the country is ruled by one royal family.

In 1900 China was ruled by the Qing family. (*There is a guide to the pronunciation of Chinese names on page 47.*) As they originally came from Manchuria, north of China, their dynasty was also known as the Manchu dynasty.

The empire which the Manchus ruled had been in existence for over 2000 years. During that time the Chinese people had become one of the most advanced civilisations in the world. They were especially skilled in astronomy, mathematics, engineering and medicine; they were the first people to use paper and had invented printing; they were making porcelain and paper long before these skills were known in the West; silk-weaving, gunpowder, spectacles, the magnetic compass and the suspension bridge were all Chinese inventions.

European influence

By 1900, however, the Chinese empire had grown weak. The main reason for this was that European countries in the nineteenth century had gained great influence in its affairs by using force against China. Between 1839 and 1842 the British fought an 'Opium War' against China to force the Chinese to continue buying the drug opium from British-ruled India. In 1860, in a second Opium War, an Anglo-French army attacked Beijing, the capital of China, and burned down government buildings. In 1894–95 the Japanese struck at China, taking away Korea, Formosa (Taiwan) and Port Arthur (Lushun). After each of these wars the invaders forced the Manchus to sign 'unequal treaties', giving them control of China's sea-ports and allowing them special trading privileges. By the end of the nineteenth century, fifty of China's ports were **treaty ports**, open to foreign trade and residence. In addition, the European powers had divided China up into what they called **spheres of influence**. This meant that in the British sphere, for example, British people had the biggest share of business, missionary work, transport, etc.

Not surprisingly, Europeans were very unpopular in China. Many Chinese blamed the Manchus for allowing China to be over-run by Europeans, and plotted to overthrow them. In 1850, for example, the Taiping Rebellion against the Manchus broke out. It lasted for fourteen years and was the worst in China's long history. Between 1850 and 1864 vast areas of fertile land were laid waste, 600 cities were ruined, and 20 million people were killed. The Manchus were only able to put down the rebellion with European help, and this made them even more unpopular.

Reforms

In 1898 the Emperor Guangxu tried to strengthen China by modernising the way the empire was run. In a three month period known as the **Hundred Days of Reform**, Guangxu introduced new schools and colleges and a new examination system. He improved the government's budget and dismissed corrupt officials from the court. However, Guangxu's aunt, the Empress Dowager Cixi, opposed these changes. Helped by conservative court officials, Cixi had the Emperor imprisoned and forced him to grant her the power to rule China in his place.

The Empress Dowager Cixi photographed on the Dragon Throne of the Manchus in 1900. Note her long fingernails protected by sheaths, a symbol of social superiority since she clearly does not have to do manual work

The Boxer Rebellion, 1900

At the time of the Hundred Days of Reform, opposition to the Manchus was common throughout China. Many opponents of the Manchus also hated foreigners, especially Christians. Their discontent reached a peak when two successive harvests failed and the Yellow River flooded huge areas of farm land, causing a famine. Discontent boiled up into rebellion.

The rebellion was organised by a movement called Yi-Ho Tuan, meaning Righteous and Harmonious Militia. Because its members practised the martial arts, including boxing, they were known as Boxers. The Boxers blamed foreigners and Christians – 'foreign devils' as they called them – for the problems of China. They especially hated Chinese converts to Christianity. At first the Boxers also opposed the Manchus, but Empress Dowager Cixi cleverly won them over to her side by giving them official support and by encouraging them to attack foreigners.

The Boxer Rebellion reached a climax in 1900. When the Boxers killed Europeans and Christians whom they had captured, European governments sent an armed force to Beijing to protect their nationals. This European force, however, was defeated by a Chinese army cooperating with the Boxers. At the same time, a Boxer rising began in Beijing itself. Boxers attacked and burnt the French cathedral there, killing hundreds of Chinese Christians in the flames. In the Legation area, where foreign embassy officials and their families lived, the Boxers trapped nearly 1000 foreigners and kept them under siege for two months.

The European governments reacted angrily to the siege of the Legations. A six-nation force invaded China, captured and looted Beijing, and forced the Manchus to pay a fine of £67 million. Many captured Boxers were executed in the streets.

The crushing of the Boxers did not solve anybody's problems. The harsh methods used by the Europeans to suppress the Boxers made many Chinese hate them even more. At the same time, the invasion and looting of Beijing once again showed how weak the Manchus were.

A Boxer about to be executed by beheading. One of many executions of Boxers in Beijing in 1900

After the Boxer Rebellion

Empress Dowager Cixi now realised that changes were necessary after all. In 1905 she began to modernise the education system. She created a New Army modelled on European armies. She promised the formation of a parliament and democratic elections. But these measures were too little and too late to save the Manchu dynasty. The anti-Manchu, anti-foreigner movement had spread to so many people that it was only a matter of time before the Manchus would be overthrown.

Work section

A. Test your understanding of this chapter by explaining what these words and terms mean:
dynasty; Manchus; 'unequal treaties'; spheres of influence; Boxers.

B. Study the photograph above. Then, using the information in this chapter as well as your own imagination, answer the following questions:
1. Name the organisation to which the condemned man belonged.
2. What were the aims of this organisation?
3. Suggest why this man was executed. Why do you think the execution was done in public?
4. Suggest what thoughts were going through the minds of the onlookers at the moment when the photograph was taken.
5. For what purposes do you think the photograph was taken? Explain your answer.

2

THE REVOLUTION OF 1911

Sun Yatsen

Many of the enemies of the Manchu dynasty in 1900 had a handsome thirty-four-year-old doctor named Sun Yatsen as their leader.

Doctor Sun was a Christian. He had been educated in American schools in Hawaii and in a British college in Hong Kong. He had spent many years travelling the world, and what he saw in advanced industrial countries like Britain and Japan made him think that China was backward and weak. Sun Yatsen came to believe that the only hope for China lay in making it a republic organised on modern, Western lines. That would mean getting rid of the Manchu dynasty which was so opposed to change.

Sun Yatsen founded several secret societies with the aim of overthrowing the Manchus by force. From 1894 to 1905 he led a 'Revive China Society' and, in 1905, he founded the 'Tongmenghui', meaning 'Sworn Chinese Brotherhood'. Doctor Sun's three aims, which he announced in 1898, were to 'Eliminate the Manchus, eliminate the monarchy: open the road to socialism'. All his attempts at revolution failed, however. By 1911 he had attempted to overthrow the government on ten separate occasions, but none had succeeded.

The last years of the Manchus

In 1908 the seventy-three-year-old Empress Dowager Cixi died. Her successor as ruler of China was her nephew, a two-year-old boy named Puyi, who was given the title of Emperor. The Manchu dynasty was clearly in trouble.

The power to rule was given to a Regent, Prince Chun, the boy's uncle. Prince Chun sided with the conservatives in the court – the politicians and princes and courtiers who disliked change. He gave important positions to his brothers and appointed the most conservative of the Imperial Princes to the post of Prime Minister. At the same time he dismissed many powerful and able officials, including the chief military commander in north China, Yuan Shikai.

In 1911 China entered a period of economic difficulty and discontent. The harvest failed in all the central areas of the country. It was the worst crop failure for forty years and caused great distress among the peasants. The wealthier classes were also discontented because the government had increased their taxes to pay for the New Army. They also disliked a government plan for building railways, using foreign loans and technical assistance.

The Wuchang rebellion

In September 1911 a rebellion against the government began in Sichuan province after police fired on a crowd of demonstrators, killing many of them. Agents of Sun Yatsen's 'Sworn Chinese Brotherhood' immediately went to Sichuan to help spread the rebellion. On 10 October – the Double Tenth, as the

A street in Beijing in October 1911 after the execution of supporters of the Manchus

rebels called the tenth day of the tenth month – soldiers of the New Army in their base at Wuchang joined the rising. With the help of the New Army the rebels quickly took control of Wuchang. From there the rebellion spread throughout central and southern China, and became a full-scale revolution. By the end of November fifteen of the country's eighteen provinces had joined the revolution. In the city of Nanjing the rebels formed a provisional government in opposition to the Manchu government in Beijing.

The Manchus tried to deal with the revolution by recalling Yuan Shikai from retirement. Yuan Shikai was made Prime Minister and Commander-in-Chief of the armies, and was ordered to crush the rebels by all possible means.

Yuan Shikai was the most able general in China, and he quickly defeated the rebels and recaptured Wuchang. But instead of punishing the rebels, he made a deal with their leaders. In return for their support, he promised to help them achieve their aims; he would use his great power and influence to persuade Prince Chun, the Regent, and Puyi, the six-year-old Emperor, to give up the throne and make China into a republic. Yuan Shikai himself would take office as President of the Republic.

The contest for leadership

While these events were taking place, Sun Yatsen was in America on a fund-raising tour. On 24 December Sun returned to China and a week later was elected President of 'The United Provinces of China' by an assembly of the rebels at Nanjing.

A contest for the leadership of China now took place between Yuan Shikai and Sun Yatsen. Sun was the democratic choice of the rebels, but Yuan had the support of the army. With this military superiority, Yuan was able to persuade the assembly in Nanjing that he, not Sun, should be President. The assembly duly elected him President in February 1912. Sun resigned without protest in order to avoid a civil war between Yuan's army and his own supporters.

Finally, on 12 February 1912, Prince Chun and Emperor Puyi stepped down from the 'Dragon Throne' of the Manchus. The Edict of Abdication which they issued said:

'Today the people of the whole Empire have their minds bent on a Republic, the southern provinces having begun the movement, and the northern generals having subsequently supported it. The will of Providence is clear and the people's wishes are plain. How could I, for the sake of the glory and honour of one family, oppose the wishes of teeming millions? Wherefore I, with the Emperor, decide that the form of government in China shall be a constitutional Republic. . .'

The Daily Mirror
THE MORNING JOURNAL WITH THE SECOND LARGEST NET SALE

| No. 2,487. | Registered at the G.P.O. as a Newspaper. | SATURDAY, OCTOBER 14, 1911 | One Halfpenny. |

PU YI, CHINA'S FIVE-YEAR-OLD EMPEROR, WHOM THE REVOLUTIONARIES ARE SEEKING TO DEPOSE.

Dr. Sun Yat Sen   The Regent and his second son.   The Emperor.

China is in the throes of a revolution, the aim of which is nothing less than the overthrow of the Manchu dynasty and the establishment of a Republic. Pu Yi, the present Emperor, who is now five and a half, came to the throne when only three years old. Ruler over 300,000,000 souls, he lives a life secluded from the world, even his mother only being allowed to pay him occasional visits. In the palace he is addressed as Wan-Sui-Yeh (Lord of Ten Thousand Years). Prince Chun, the Regent, is the little Emperor's father. Dr. Sun Yat Sen is named as the President of the first Republic—if it is established.

Work section

A. Study the Edict of Abdication above. Then, using the information you have read in this chapter, answer the following questions:
 1. Who were 'I' (line 7), 'one family' (line 7–8) and 'the Emperor' (line 9)?
 2. In which of the 'southern provinces' did the movement for a Republic start? In which city was a Republican government set up?
 3. Name the leading 'northern general' who later supported the Republican movement.
 4. Explain in your own words the meaning of the term 'constitutional Republic'. In what ways does a constitutional republic differ from a monarchy?

B. Study the front page of the Daily Mirror above, then answer these questions:
 1. Why do you think the Daily Mirror gave the whole of its front page to this story?
 2. Who was 'Dr Sun Yat-sen' in the bottom left? Why do you think the last sentence of the newspaper report expresses doubt that he would become President of the first Chinese Republic?

WARLORD CHINA, 1912–27

The Presidency of Yuan Shikai, 1912–16

The 'constitutional republic' set up in 1912 was meant to be a democracy, with an elected parliament sharing the tasks of government with President Yuan Shikai. Accordingly, elections for a parliament known as the **National Assembly** were held in 1913.

In the elections of 1913 a new party set up by Sun Yatsen won a majority of seats in the National Assembly. This was the People's National Party, or **Guomindang**. However, Yuan Shikai was not interested in sharing power with a parliament dominated by Sun Yatsen's party. He quickly began to ignore the Assembly's decisions, expecially when it proved to be inefficient, corrupt and slow to make decisions. Yuan clearly intended to govern China as a dictator, not as a democrat.

In January 1914 Yuan Shikai dissolved the National Assembly after making himself President for the next ten years and giving himself wide powers. At the same time he gained the support of the major European powers which wanted a strong government in China to protect their trading interests there. By the end of 1914 Yuan was ruling as a dictator and twelve of the eighteen provinces were under his control. Military governors in these provinces made sure that they stayed loyal to Yuan.

A Chinese postcard of 1912 showing Yuan Shikai in military uniform. Behind him is the new flag of Republican China – five stripes of red, yellow, blue, white and black, representing the five main peoples of China: Chinese, Manchus, Mongols, Muslims, and Tibetans.

By 1915 Yuan felt confident enough to make himself Emperor. It was an ancient Chinese tradition that a strong general who overthrew a weak emperor, as Yuan had done, should unite China under his own rule and found a new dynasty. In December 1915 Yuan accepted what the ancient Chinese called 'the mandate of heaven' – that is, the right of the Emperor to rule 'all the land that lies under heaven'. He planned to call his dynasty 'The Grand Constitutional Era' – the twenty-seventh in China's 2000-year history.

Three groups of people opposed Yuan's plan to become Emperor. One was Sun Yatsen's new party, the Guomindang, which wanted a democratic government. Another consisted of the generals in Yuan's army and the military governors of the provinces; they feared that they would lose authority if Yuan had more power. And the third was the Japanese government which had plans to bring large areas of China under its control (see Chapter 7).

Early in 1915 the Japanese government presented Yuan with **Twenty-One Demands**, demanding control of many of China's factories, railways and ports, and threatening war if the demands were refused. The Chinese people were naturally outraged by the Twenty-One Demands, and when Yuan accepted many of them rather than go to war with Japan, he quickly lost popularity. On Christmas Day 1915 the army in remote Yunnan province rebelled against him. Other army garrisons in neighbouring provinces joined the revolt. Faced with the opposition of the army which had brought him to power in the first place, Yuan dropped his plans to become Emperor. Shortly after, in June 1916, he died of a stroke – though most people said it was really of a broken heart.

The warlords

Yuan Shikai had managed to hold China together under his rule, but after his death there was no one leader popular enough to command the loyalty of all the Chinese. The result was the collapse of the central government in Beijing. For the next eleven years, from 1916 to 1927, it only controlled a small area around Beijing. In the south the Guomindang, under their leader Sun Yatsen, set up a rival government in Guangzhou. In other areas the generals and the military governors who had opposed Yuan set up their own governments and used their armies to enforce their authority. These men were the **warlords**.

From 1916 onwards the warlords fought each other for control of China. The greatest warlords governed whole provinces (see map). Within the provinces under their control, groups of generals and officers controlled smaller areas – cities and counties, for example – and were warlords in their own right. There were hundreds of warlords, and most were interested only in their own power and wealth, not in helping the people under their rule. They imposed high taxes, enlisted peasants into their armies, and governed with great severity.

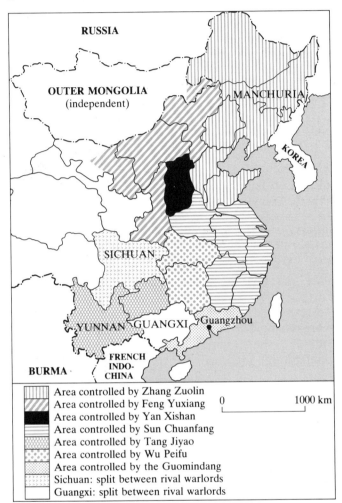

China under the warlords, 1916–27

The strictness of warlord rule can be glimpsed in this extract from an article written in 1927 by a French journalist about an interview she had with Marshal Zhang Zuolin, the warlord of Manchuria:

A. '. . . A small fat man with a jovial and crafty countenance . . . shook hands with me and bade me welcome in impeccable French. "The Marshal will receive you shortly. We are preparing an offensive, and he is still in conference with his generals. But I am going to let him know you are here. I am M. Wuching (Foreign Minister)."

To kill time, we struck up a conversation. "What do you think of our capital, and of our streets? The Marshal, you know, insists on cleanliness and order."

The city, I must say, was well policed. I remember seeing two heads, still dripping with blood, swaying in a fisherman's net by the door of a theatre: two soldiers had been executed there for having disregarded the law that forbade them to enter without paying.

M. Wuching probably read my thoughts: "What else could we do? Stern punishments are salutary warnings to any mutineers. Pity is unforgivable when it comes to setting an example . . . Do drink your tea please, and have a cigarette."'

Conditions in China were worst when the warlords fought each other to get control of each other's provinces. The largest of these civil wars took place in 1920 and 1922, and involved up to 300,000 soldiers. In these wars, both sides fought with great ferocity and cruelty. This extract from the memoirs of the British Consul in the city of Chengdu gives us an idea of the horrors of the war. It is about an attack by Yunnanese soldiers on Chengdu in 1920.

B. 'Seven hundred Yunnan men stripped; some were entirely naked, some naked to the waist. Armed with knives and revolvers they rushed the Sichuan camp of 16,000 men at the foot of the hills. The attack was a complete success. Panic seized regiment after regiment and the whole force fled . . .

About ten of these heroes . . . were captured and, naked as they were, kept in the streets on show in cold drenching rain before being murdered. Two were killed and cut up in the streets, and I saw the hearts and livers in a cookshop.'

Work section

A. Test your understanding of this chapter by explaining what the following words and terms mean: National Assembly; Guomindang; the Twenty-One Demands; warlords.

B. Study source A above. Then, using the information in this chapter, answer these questions:
1. For what reasons do you think the marshal was 'preparing an offensive'?
2. For what offence had two soldiers been beheaded?
3. Why, according to Monsieur Wuching, were they executed for this offence?

C. Study the map above, then answer these questions:
1. Which warlord appears from the map to have been the most powerful?
2. How powerful does the Guomindang appear to have been? Explain your answer.

4

THE NEW REVOLUTIONARIES

During the years of warlord rule after 1916, many young Chinese joined revolutionary groups and parties, hoping to improve their country.

The May Fourth movement

The first was a protest movement against the peace treaties which ended the Great War of 1914–18. It began on 4 May 1919 and is therefore known as the May Fourth movement.

China had joined the Great War in 1917 on the side of the Western Allies. Nine hundred thousand Chinese labourers went to France, Turkey and Africa to work for the Allied armies in 'Labour Battalions'. German ships at anchor in Chinese ports were seized, and German businesses were closed and confiscated.

At the end of the war Chinese representatives took part in the Paris Peace Conference. One of the issues under discussion was the future of Germany's possessions in China, for, until 1914, Germany had enjoyed special rights in the port of Kiaochow (see map on page 16). At the start of the war the Japanese had seized Kiaochow from the Germans. And in 1915 they had tried to increase their influence in China by presenting Yuan Shikai with Twenty-One Demands (see page 6).

At the Paris Peace Conference the Chinese expected Kiaochow to be returned to them. They expected Japan to withdraw the Twenty-One Demands, and they also wanted an end to the 'unequal treaties' (see page 2). In the event, China gained none of these things. The peacemakers decided that Japan could keep Kiaochow, and it did nothing to end the 'unequal treaties'.

When news of the Paris Peace Conference reached China, protests and demonstrations began. On 4 May 1919 around 10,000 Beijing students and school pupils organised a massive demonstration. This student rebellion quickly spread throughout the country. Strikes, demonstrations and a boycott of Japanese goods kept China in a state of unrest for the whole of May 1919.

The May Fourth movement added strength to a revolution in ideas known as the **New Tide** which had already begun in 1916. Led by a group of teachers at Beijing University, the New Tide aimed to get rid of old-fashioned ideas and to introduce modern ideas of freedom, equal rights and scientific progress. The New Tide also aimed to simplify China's complex language so that poor and uneducated people could read about the new ideas in magazines and newspapers. And although the thinkers of the New Tide wanted an end to foreign control in China, they were perfectly willing to use foreign ideas to achieve their aims.

The Communists and the Guomindang

One set of foreign ideas that found its way into China was Communism – a movement begun by Karl Marx and his followers in the nineteenth century, which aims to create a classless society in which most property is commonly owned. In 1918 an assistant librarian at Beijing University named Mao Zedong helped set up a 'Society for the Study of Marxism'. The Society's meetings were well-attended and, in 1921, its members set up a **Chinese Communist Party**.

Meanwhile, in Guangzhou, Sun Yatsen was reorganising his party, the Guomindang. Since 1917 Sun and the Guomindang had been in control of Guangdong province in the south. In 1924 he announced that the policy of the Guomindang was based on **Three Principles:** national freedom; democratic government; and the people's livelihood. His aim was to unite China under his leadership and make it into a republic free from foreign interference.

To achieve his aims, Sun Yatsen needed foreign help against the warlords who controlled so much of China. However, the Western powers such as Britain refused to support him. Sun therefore turned to the USSR where a Communist government had come to power in 1917. The Russian government gave support to Sun in 1922 by sending one of its most able diplomats, Abram Joffe, to help him reorganise the Guomindang.

With Abram Joffe's help, Sun Yatsen reorganised the Guomindang on Russian Communist lines. It became a mass party, run with strict discipline, with individual members having to show total obedience to party decisions. In addition, Sun agreed that members of the Chinese Communist Party could also belong to the Guomindang. For although the aims of the two parties were different, they both wanted a revolution, and joint membership would allow them to work together to achieve this. There followed several years of active cooperation between the two parties.

In 1923 the Russian government sent two more agents, Michael Borodin and General Galen, to help Sun improve the Guomindang. General Galen's job was to help create a Guomindang army strong enough to beat the warlords and conquer the rest of China. He sold Sun Russian rifles and he set up a military

A Guomindang poster of 1926 shows the recently deceased Sun Yatsen (top) and Chiang Kaishek (below, on horseback) leading the Guomindang armies in the Northern Campaign of 1926–7

academy at Huangpu to train the officers who would lead the army. In charge of the Huangpu academy was Sun's brother-in-law, Chiang Kaishek.

Chiang Kaishek and the Northern Campaign

In March 1925 Sun Yatsen died of cancer. While the other Guomindang leaders argued with each other about who should take his place, Chiang Kaishek became Commander-in-Chief of the new Guomindang army. By this time, his military academy at Huangpu had turned out 500 trained officers, so he could now begin the enormous task of conquering and unifying China.

In July 1926 Chiang Kaishek began a **March to the North** at the head of the Guomindang armies. Ahead of him he sent political agents to whip up support among ordinary people by promising a 'national revolution' and a 'new order' in China. Millions of Chinese, sick of warlord rule, gladly supported him.

One of the Guomindang armies, led by Communist officers, quickly captured Hankow and set up a government there in September 1926. Another Guomindang army captured Nanjing early in 1927 and set up a Nationalist government. There was little actual fighting and the March to the North was easier than Chiang had expected. In some cases, warlords had to surrender to him because their armies mutinied and joined the Guomindang. In many areas, poor peasants and workers welcomed Chiang's armies because they believed the propaganda which promised better times ahead. And in areas where there was no enthusiasm for the Guomindang, Chiang did not hesitate to use cash to win support through bribery.

The Communist-Guomindang split

Now that the Communists and the Guomindang had extended their influence north and conquered all of southern China, the alliance between them broke down.

As the Guomindang armies approached Shanghai and prepared to attack it, the workers of Shanghai rebelled against the warlord who ruled the area. The rebellion was led by Communists under Zhou Enlai, who set up a Communist council to run the city. When Chiang Kaishek's army arrived several days later, it took over the streets of Shanghai, rounded up all the Communists it could find, and killed them. Later in the year, Chiang's men also crushed the Communists in Guangzhou, executing hundreds of them in the streets and forcing thousands more to flee for their lives.

After being expelled from the cities, the Communists retreated to the countryside in Jiangxi and Hunan provinces (see map on page 13). Chiang Kaishek, in control of the cities and at the head of the government in Nanjing, now got ready to conquer the rest of China.

Work section

A. Test your understanding of this chapter by explaining what the following mean: the May Fourth movement; the New Tide; the Three Principles of the Guomindang; the March to the North.

B. Study the poster above, then answer these questions:
1. What impression does the artist give of the Guomindang armies?
2. What do you think were the aims of the artist in drawing this poster?
3. Judging by the information in this chapter, how accurate do you think this picture of the Guomindang is? Explain your answer.

5

CONQUEST AND EXTERMINATION, 1928–34

The unification of China, 1928

In April 1928 the leaders of the Guomindang put Chiang Kaishek in command of a second Northern Campaign. His orders were to go much further north and capture Beijing, the capital, and thus bring northern China under Guomindang control.

To strengthen his army Chiang Kaishek made an alliance with two powerful warlords in the north – Feng Yuxiang whose army numbered 300,000 men, and Yan Xishan. With their help, Chiang was able to fight a war against the most powerful warlord of all – Zhang Zuolin, the ruler of Manchuria, who had parts of northern China, including Beijing, under his control.

After a short campaign, Chiang Kaishek's forces entered Beijing. Their task was made easier when a bomb exploded on the train taking Zhang Zuolin out of the city, killing him. Zhang's successor as warlord of Manchuria, his son Zhang Xueliang, surrendered to Chiang Kaishek and recognised the Guomindang as the true government of united China.

The Guomindang was now the most powerful single force in China. It transferred the capital from Beijing to its base in Nanjing, in the richest part of the country. There it set itself up as the **National Government** and gave the power to rule to a Council of State. The Chairman of this Council was Chiang Kaishek, making him, in effect, the ruler of China.

Disunity

In reality, Chiang Kaishek had not by any means united China under his rule. He had only managed to conquer the north with the help of the local warlords, Feng Yuxiang and Yan Xishan, and they had never fully accepted his authority. In 1929 Feng and Yan rebelled against Chiang. For the next two years, northern China suffered a violent and bloody civil war as Chiang fought Feng and Yan to regain control. Even when Yan Xishan was defeated he was able to retreat to Shanxi province and set up his own government there.

Even in provinces that were theoretically under his rule, Chiang Kaishek did not always have real control. A major problem was the existence of large gangs of bandits which terrorised whole districts and existed by looting, kidnapping and theft. An official Chinese report made in 1929, about bandit gangs in the Mienchih district, gives us an idea of the scale of the problem:

A. 'When they capture a person for ransom they first pierce his legs with iron wire, and bind them together as fish are hung on a string. When they returned to their bandit dens, the captives were interrogated and were pricked with sickles to make them tell of hidden property they possessed. If there was the slightest hesitation in answering, they were immediately cut in two at the waist – as a warning to others. Then they compelled the villagers to disclose where was hidden the little store of grain with which they were trying to eke out [make] an existence. This they carried off, leaving the victims to starve. If any of the adults tried to escape the whole family was slaughtered . . .

In many cases in Mienchih there will be found only eight or ten houses left standing in towns which a year ago had 400 or 450 houses. What has become of the families which once lived in the demolished homes, no man can tell.'

The Jiangxi Soviet

Another area of China which Chiang Kaishek did not control was the province of Jiangxi.

As you have read, the alliance between the Communists and the Guomindang broke down in 1927, and the Communists were thrown out of the big cities with great bloodshed. The survivors of these massacres retreated into the countryside, most of them to Jiangxi province where they set up a 'Chinese Soviet Republic', generally known as the **Jiangxi Soviet**, to govern the province. Mao Zedong was their political leader while Zhu De led the armed forces of the Soviet.

Within a few years of arriving in Jiangxi the Communists had gained the support of many of the peasants living under their rule. This was largely because a Land Law which the Communists passed in 1930 divided up all the cultivated land among the farming population. Millions of peasants who had never before owned land now found they were their own masters. As well as redistributing the land, the Communists reduced the taxes on land, set up schools, abolished outmoded practices such as arranged marriages, and created Peasant Councils to allow communities a say in the running of their affairs.

The Communist **Red Army** also played an important part in winning the support of the peasants. The Red Army's rules of discipline help to explain how it did this:

B. '1 Replace all doors when you leave a house [*doors in peasant homes were on hooks, not hinges*];
2 Return and roll up the straw matting on which you sleep;
3 Be courteous and polite to the people and help them when you can;
4 Return all borrowed articles;
5 Replace all damaged articles;
6 Be honest in all transactions with the peasants;
7 Pay for all articles purchased;
8 Be sanitary and, especially, establish latrines a safe distance from people's houses.'

The extermination campaigns, 1930–4

Chiang Kaishek regarded the Jiangxi Soviet as a greater threat to his authority than either the warlords or bandits. He therefore organised a series of 'extermination campaigns' against the Communists in an attempt to wipe them out.

Between 1930 and 1934 Chiang Kaishek mounted five extermination campaigns, each one bigger than the last. But although his armies always outnumbered the Communists, the first four campaigns were total failures. This was because Mao Zedong and Zhu De used clever tactics to fight them: instead of fighting them head-on in pitched battles, they lured the Guomindang armies deep into Communist-held territory and then attacked each unit separately, knocking them out in deadly ambushes. Mao summed up these tactics in four slogans:

Guomindang troops setting out on an extermination campaign against the Communists in 1930

C. '1 When the enemy advances, we retreat!
2 When the enemy halts and encamps, we trouble them!
3 When the enemy seeks to avoid a battle, we attack!
4 When the enemy retreats, we pursue!'

There was, however, a major drawback to Mao's tactics. Whenever he lured Guomindang units into Communist-held areas, they were able to capture Communist villages as they advanced. In the four years of the extermination campaigns, more than a million peasants were killed or starved to death as a result. Understandably, many members of the Communist Party criticised Mao's tactics, saying that not only were they politically wrong; they were also cowardly.

Work section

A. Test your understanding of this chapter by explaining what the following terms mean: the Jiangxi Soviet; the Red Army; extermination campaigns.

B. Study source A, then answer these questions:
1. Why do you think the bandits treated their captives with such cruelty?
2. Suggest what might have caused the destruction of so many homes in the district.
3. How does the report show that Chiang Kaishek had no authority in the area?

C. Study source B, then answer these questions:
1. What light do these rules of discipline throw on the behaviour of other Chinese armies? Explain your answer in detail.
2. What do you think were the aims of these rules of discipline?

D. Study the photograph above, then answer these questions:
1. In what ways do the Guomindang soldiers look well-equipped for fighting the Communists? How might their equipment cause them difficulties?
2. Compare the photograph with the poster on page 9. How does the Guomindang military strength shown in the photograph differ from the impression created by the poster?

E. Judging by what you have read in this chapter, why do you think that Chiang Kaishek saw the Communists in Jiangxi as a greater threat than either the warlords or bandits?

THE LONG MARCH

The fifth campaign

In autumn 1933 Chiang Kaishek launched his fifth and biggest extermination campaign against the Communists. This time he used a new method of attack worked out by a military adviser from Germany, General Hans von Seeckt.

Instead of invading the Red areas and trying to capture them by fighting battles, Seeckt's method was to surround the Jiangxi Soviet with half a million troops who then advanced very slowly, building blockhouses (*concrete shelters*), digging trenches and putting up barbed wire fences as they went. Seeckt's aim was to stop all movement into and out of the Soviet, starving the Communists of food, fuel, weapons and ammunition, and slowly reducing the area they controlled.

Seeckt's 'blockhouse strategy' was very successful. By October 1934 the Communists had lost over half their territory, 60,000 soldiers in the Red Army had been killed, and the area under their control was steadily shrinking as the Guomindang advanced.

New Communist tactics

As you have read, the Communists survived the first four extermination campaigns by luring Guomindang units into their territory, and then smashing them in concentrated attacks. In the fifth campaign, however, they adopted different tactics.

The new tactics were suggested by a Russian agent who had been sent to advise the Jiangxi Soviet by the Russian government. His name was Otto Braun. Braun insisted that Mao Zedong's tactics were politically wrong: the Red Army should not retreat and allow peasants to be captured and killed by the Guomindang, he said. Instead, the Red Army should defend the borders of the Soviet by fighting head-on battles with the Guomindang.

Backed by twenty-four Russian-trained leaders of the Jiangxi Soviet, Otto Braun got his way. Mao Zedong's tactics were abandoned and Mao was expelled from the Party's Central Committee. Under Braun's leadership, the Red Army now began to defend its territory in pitched battles – but at great cost. In the Battle of Guanchang in April 1934 the Red Army lost 8000 men. And with the Guomindang's blockhouse rings cutting them off from the rest of China, they could not easily replace these men or their weapons.

By the summer of 1934 the Red Army was completely caged into Jiangxi, surrounded by four lines of blockhouses. Mao Zedong suggested that the Red Army should try to break through these lines to attack the Guomindang from the rear. But Otto Braun and the Russian-trained leaders of the Soviet rejected Mao's advice. Instead they planned a retreat: the Red Army would try to break through the blockhouse lines and then head for the Communist base on the Hunan-Hubei border where their Second Army Group was based (see map opposite.)

The Long March

On 16 October 1934 some 87,000 soldiers of the Red Army set out on the retreat planned by Otto Braun.

As they retreated, the Reds took with them all the equipment of the Jiangxi Soviet that would be needed for setting up a new government in Hunan-Hubei. Thousands of bearers carried office furniture, files, a printing press, radio equipment, gold bars, telephone wire, and so on. In addition, the Army took with it as much weaponry and ammunition as it could carry: 33,000 guns, 1,800,000 cartridges, 76,000 grenades, 38 mortars and 25,000 mortar shells.

It took the Red Army six weeks to break through the blockhouse rings encircling Jiangxi. But no sooner had they broken through than they were forced to fight a major battle when they reached the Xiang River (25 November-3 December). By the end of the battle, the Red Army had lost 45,000 men, more than half the number which had set out from Jiangxi.

Many of the Red Army commanders blamed Otto Braun for their great losses of men. The losses had been due partly to the amount of equipment they were carrying, which slowed them down, giving the Guomindang time to prepare attacks. Second, Otto Braun was leading the Red Army in a straight line, making it easy for the Guomindang to predict its movements.

When the Red Army reached the town of Zunyi on 9 January 1935, the leaders of the Communist Party held a meeting to work out better tactics. At the Zunyi Conference Otto Braun was suspended and military control of the Red Army was given back to Mao Zedong and Zhu De.

Mao takes control

Under the leadership of Mao and Zhu, the Red Army now took a new direction – or rather, a series of directions. Twisting and turning, splitting into groups and reforming, it now went south from Zunyi, swung round through remote Yunnan province before crossing the wide River Yangzi into Sichuan province. The Army's new destination was Shaanxi province in northern China where another Soviet had control of the Yanan district.

As they trekked north, the Red Army faced many

great obstacles and carried out many daring acts. One of the most famous of these was the crossing of the Dadu River, when twenty-two soldiers swung across the river gorge on chains – all that was left of the suspension bridge across it – while under enemy fire. Their heroic action made it possible for the rest of the Red Army to cross the river.

The **Long March** of the Red Army took it over the Snowy Mountains – among the highest in the world – and through the treacherous Grasslands where hundreds of men drowned in deep marshes. Along much of the route they were continually harassed by the Guomindang, by local warlords and by hostile non-Chinese tribesmen.

The Long March came to an end when the Red Army reached Yanan in October 1935. Fewer than 10,000 of those who had set out marched into Yanan. Over 9000 kilometres and 368 days of marching, hunger, enemy attack, disease, exposure, accidents and desertion had seen to the rest. However, the arrival of the Second and Fourth Front Armies which had undertaken their own long marches (see map) quickly restored the Red Army's strength to 80,000 men, making it once again a viable fighting force.

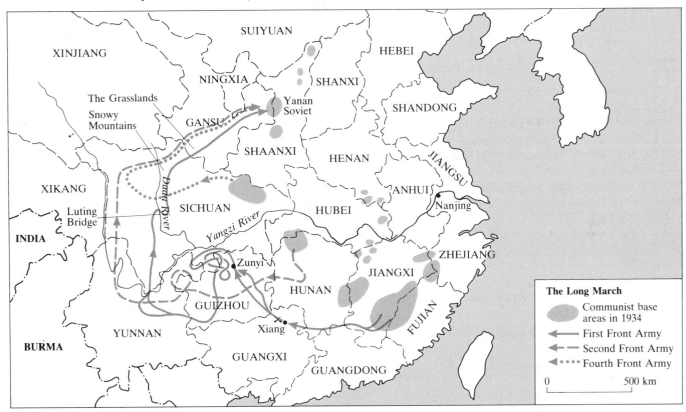

The route of the Long March

Work section

A. Study the map above, then answer these questions:
    1. Describe in your own words the Red Army's movements in between Jiangxi and Zunyi.
    2. Describe how the Red Army's movements changed after leaving Zunyi.
    3. Judging by what you have read in this chapter, why do you think the Army changed its movements in this way?
    4. What might have been the result if the Red Army had not changed direction at Zunyi?

B. Read these comments on the Long March, then answer the questions which follow.

    A. 'Less than 20,000 survivors of the Long March reached the Shaanxi base . . . Chinese Communism had suffered a severe, but by no means decisive defeat at the hands of the Nationalists. As for the latter, their success since the launching of the 1928 Northern Campaign had been remarkable.'

    B. 'The Long March proclaims to the world that the Red Army is an army of heroes and that Chiang Kaishek and his like are perfect nonentities. It announces the bankruptcy of the encirclement, pursuit, obstruction and interception attempted by Chiang Kaishek.'

    1. Using the information in this chapter, provide evidence to agree and disagree with each of the views expressed in sources A and B.
    2. In the light of the evidence you have found, which of the two views do you think is more accurate? Explain your answer.

Revision guide

This is an outline of the main points. It is not a complete set of notes to be copied. You should make your own notes under the headings suggested, taking your information from pages 2 to 13.

A. China in 1900
1. The Manchu dynasty
2. Foreign interference in China in the nineteenth century
3. Opposition to Manchus and foreigners
   a) The Taiping Rebellion
   b) The Boxer Rebellion, 1900
4. Attempts at reform
   a) The Hundred Days of Reform, 1898
   b) Empress Dowager Cixi's reforms

B. The revolution of 1911
1. Sun Yatsen
2. The last years of the Manchus, 1908–11
3. The Wuchang Rebellion
4. The contest for leadership between Yuan Shikai and Sun Yatsen
5. China becomes a Republic, 1912

C. Warlord China
1. The Presidency of Yuan Shikai, 1912–16
2. The rule of the warlords, 1916–27

D. The new revolutionaries
1. The May Fourth movement
2. The New Tide
3. The Chinese Communist Party
4. The Guomindang
   a) The Three Principles
   b) Its organisation
   c) Its links with the Communist Party

E. The Northern Campaign, 1926–7
1. Chiang Kaishek's March to the North
2. The Guomindang-Communist split, 1927

F. The unification of China
1. The second Northern Campaign, 1928
2. The creation of the 'National Government'.

G. Continuing disunity
1. Problems with warlords
2. Bandit gangs
3. The Jiangxi Soviet

H. The extermination campaigns, 1930–4
1. The first four campaigns
2. The fifth campaign

I. The Long March, 1934–5
1. Reasons why the Communists left Jiangxi
2. The retreat to Zunyi
3. The Zunyi Conference
4. The Long March to Yanan
5. Results of the Long March

PART
TWO

CHINA AT WAR

The rising sun over the Great Wall of China in 1937. The Great Wall was built in the third century BC to keep out invaders. Here a Japanese sentry on the dawn watch, with his country's 'rising sun' flag in one hand, looks out over Japanese-occupied north China

While Chiang Kaishek was trying to wipe out the Communists in the extermination campaigns of 1930–5, he himself was under attack from another direction: Japan.

A glance at the map on page 16 will show you that Japan is an island nation lying in the Pacific Ocean to the east of China, and very much smaller than China.

At the start of this century Japan was well on the way to becoming one of the world's major powers. Its population, its industry, and its military and naval strength were all growing fast. This rapid growth, however, created a problem: being an island nation,

Japan did not have enough space for its growing population, nor enough food for it, nor enough raw materials for its factories.

The obvious solution to this problem was to do the same as the Western powers had done in the nineteenth century; that is, to grab land overseas and make an empire to provide itself with raw materials, trade outlets and room for expansion.

In Part Two we will find out how Japan's attempt to create an overseas empire involved China in war for fifteen years, and took the lives of countless millions of Chinese people.

THE THREAT FROM JAPAN

Japanese expansion

As you have read (page 2) Japan fought a war with China in 1895 in order to get Chinese land. As a result of the war China had to give Formosa (now called Taiwan) and the Pescadores Islands to Japan, and to allow Korea, one of its colonies, independence.

Japan gained more land in China after fighting a war with Russia in 1904–5 for control of Manchuria and Korea. Both countries already owned railways, ports and factories in Manchuria and Korea; and now, as a result of winning the war, Japan gained control of the Liaodong Peninsula and the South Manchurian Railway. Five years later, in 1910, Japanese troops moved into Korea and made it a Japanese colony.

During the Great War of 1914–18 Japan grabbed even more land from China. As soon as the war began, Japan entered it on the side of the Western Allies and took control of the German-held port at Kiaochow. Then, in 1915, the Japanese government presented China with Twenty-One Demands, trying to increase its economic control of Manchuria (see page 6).

Manchuria

Manchuria was the part of China which Japan wanted above all the others. The attractions of Manchuria were clearly described by the Prime Minister of Japan, Baron Tanaka, in a letter to the Emperor of Japan:

▨	Land gained in 1895
▦	Land gained in 1905
⬚	Land gained in 1910
▤	Land gained in 1914
▥	Land gained in 1931
+++	South Manchurian Railway

0   1000 km

The expansion of Japan, 1895–1931

'It is an area of 192,000 square kilometres, having a population of 28 million people. The territory is more than three times as large as our own empire, not counting Korea and Formosa, but it is inhabited by only one third as many people. The attractiveness of the land does not arise from the scarcity of the population alone; its wealth of forestry, minerals and agricultural products is also unrivalled elsewhere in the world. In order to exploit these resources . . . we created especially the South Manchurian Railway Company.

The total investment involved in our undertakings in railways, shipping, mining, forestry, steel manufacture, agriculture, and in cattle raising . . . amount to no less than 440 million yen. It is veritably the largest single investment and the strongest organisation of our country.'

By 1927, the year in which Baron Tanaka wrote that letter, the Japanese had a stranglehold on Manchuria's economy. They controlled all its most important mines, railways, factories and ports. To protect these investments, the Japanese kept a large army in Kwantung in southern Manchuria. And to make their position even stronger, the Japanese had a friendly agreement with the warlord of Manchuria, Zhang Zuolin. They were happy to let a warlord rule Manchuria because this weakened the central government in Beijing – and a weak Chinese government suited Japan's interests very nicely.

Japan's control of Manchuria was threatened in 1928 when Chiang Kaishek marched into Beijing and set up the National Government with himself at its head. When Zhang Zuolin agreed shortly after to recognise Chiang's authority, the Japanese began to fear that Zhang and Chiang would together be strong enough to oppose their domination of Manchuria. To prevent this from happening, two Japanese colonels assassinated Zhang by dynamiting his private train. They expected that his son and successor Zhang Xueliang, a high-living, gambling drug-addict, would be easy for them to control.

Japanese soldiers of the Kwantung Army guard a street in Shenyang in 1931

A Japanese photograph of the damage to the South Manuchurian Railway

The Manchurian Incident, 1931

Having control of Manchuria's economy and of Zhang Xueliang did not solve any of Japan's basic economic problems. By 1931 the Japanese economy was in desperate trouble. The Great Depression which began in the USA had shattered Japan's trade, closed half its factories, and ruined millions of peasants. When the government proved incapable of overcoming the Depression, young officers in the Japanese army began to talk of foreign conquest as a way out of the Depression. With new colonies, they argued, Japan would have more trade, more raw materials, and more jobs. And where better to start than Manchuria, where Japan already had an army in place?

Acting against the orders of the Japanese government, officers in the Kwantung Army planned a military take-over of Manchuria. In the night of 18 September 1931 the Kwantung Army occupied the town of Shenyang, claiming that Chinese soldiers had tried to blow up the Japanese-owned South Manchurian Railway just north of the town. Ignoring the protests of the League of Nations, 50,000 Japanese soldiers went on to occupy the rest of Manchuria.

Zhang Xueliang, who by now had cured himself of drug addiction, and was proving to be an effective military governor of Manchuria, wanted to fight the Japanese invaders. But Chiang Kaishek, at the head of the new National Government, favoured relying on the League of Nations to stop the invasion. Neither he nor Zhang had the strength to fight Japan, he argued.

The League of Nations set up a Commission of Inquiry to investigate Japan's invasion but did not take any military action against Japan. While the Commission was still travelling to China by sea, the Japanese went on to occupy all of Manchuria. In February 1932 they renamed it Manzhouguo, meaning Manchu Land, and put the ex-Emperor of China, Puyi, on the throne. But Puyi was only a figure-head. The real rulers of Manzhouguo were the Japanese officers of the Kwantung Army.

Work section

A. Study Baron Tanaka's letter opposite, then answer these questions:
1. Why, according to Baron Tanaka, were the Japanese attracted to Manchuria?
2. According to Baron Tanaka, in what economic activities were the Japanese involved in Manchuria?
3. What Japanese-owned company organised all these activities?

B. Study the photograph of the damaged railway above, then answer these questions:
1. How seriously does the railway seem to be damaged?
2. For what purposes do you think the Japanese took this photograph?
3. Why do you think the Japanese reacted to the alleged attack on the railway so strongly?

C. 'When Japan invaded Manchuria in 1931 it was not really much of a surprise.' Judging by what you have read in this chapter, and by the map opposite, what evidence can you find to support this opinion?

FROM MANCHURIA TO A UNITED FRONT, 1931–7

Japan's hunger for land in China was not satisfied by the conquest of Manchuria. In 1933 the Kwantung Army occupied the province of Rehe (see map opposite) and in 1934 continued to advance slowly southwards. By the end of 1936 it had occupied the provinces of Chahaer and Suiyuan as well as parts of Hebei and Shanxi, and was demanding the separation of northern China from the south.

Chinese reactions

How did the Chinese people react to Japan's seizure of so much of their territory?

As you have read, anti-foreign feeling had been strong in China since the nineteenth century. This long-standing hatred of foreigners was now directed against the Japanese. In Shanghai, China's busiest port which handled most of its trade with Japan, Chinese people organised a boycott of Japanese goods. The effects of the boycott can be judged from this report by an American journalist in Shanghai:

A. 'No longer did the Chinese buy Japanese toys and bicycles and phonograph records. No longer did Chinese firms handle Japanese merchandise. Those who had ordered Japanese goods a few weeks ago now declined to accept them. Chinese banks refused to honor Japanese bills of lading even when the necessary funds had been deposited before. Japanese commodities piled up on Shanghai's piers, clogged the go-downs [*warehouses*]. More than 700,000 tons of cargo had been rejected and could not be disposed of. Japanese shipping went dead . . . When a Japanese ship was in port Chinese pickets would prevent Chinese passengers from boarding it or would go after them and throw them overboard. Whoever was caught buying anything "made in Japan" was summarily dealt with.'

Not surprisingly, many Chinese people wanted Chiang Kaishek to declare war on Japan and drive the Kwantung Army out of China. But Chiang Kaishek did not agree. He believed that national unity must be achieved before attacking the Japanese invaders. In other words, the Guomindang must establish its power over all of China – and that would mean wiping out the Communists – before risking a major war against Japan.

The Communists, for their part, wanted to fight Japan. They said that all Chinese people should unite to defend the nation. 'Chinese do not fight Chinese' was their main slogan in 1935. And because the Long

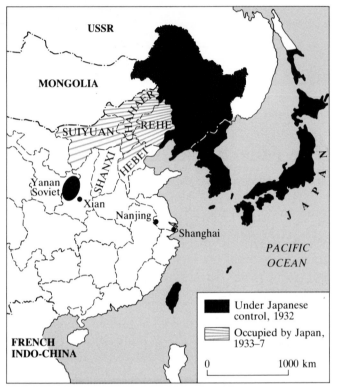

The expansion of Japan, 1931–7

March of 1934–5 had brought them close to the areas most threatened by Japan (see map above) they were in a good position to make war against Japan.

Another extermination campaign, 1936

Chiang Kaishek ignored the demands of the Communists for a 'united front' of all the Chinese against Japan. In 1936 he organised yet another extermination campaign against the Communists and sent his North-Eastern Army to attack their base in Yanan.

The base for the extermination campaign was the city of Xian, capital of Shaanxi province. The North-Eastern Army there was commanded by Zhang Xueliang who, as you have read, was driven out of Manchuria by the Japanese in 1931. His orders were to wipe out the Yanan Soviet, and bomber aircraft, tanks, armoured cars, and poison gas were all made available for his use. However, Zhang's troops were mostly Manchurians who wanted to fight the Japanese more than they wanted to fight the Communists. Zhang himself wanted revenge against the Japanese for the murder of his father.

In 1936 Zhang and the Communists made an unofficial agreement not to fight each other. They

A Japanese poster of the 1930s encouraging Japanese people to emigrate to Manchuria by showing the kind of life they might expect to find there

agreed instead to concentrate their energy on attacking the Japanese. In December 1936, however, Chiang Kaishek found out what was going on, and flew to Xian to persuade Zhang to renew the extermination campaign.

The Xian Incident, December 1936

Shortly after Chiang's arrival in Xian, something happened to make him change his mind about a 'united front': Zhang Xueliang took him prisoner.

In the early morning of 12 December 1936, 200 of Zhang's troops, led by Captain Sun Mingzhiu, stormed the hotel in which Chiang was staying. Chiang managed to escape but was soon caught hiding among rocks on the hillside behind the hotel. Captain Sun later described Chiang's capture to a British journalist who then wrote this account of it:

B. 'Sun Mingzhiu hailed him, and the Generalissimo's first words were, "If you are my comrade, shoot me and finish it all". To which Sun replied, "We will not shoot. We only ask you to lead our country against Japan . . ."

"The past is the past", Sun said to him. "From now on there must be a new policy for China. What are you going to do? . . . The one urgent task for China is to fight Japan. This is the special demand of the men of the North-East. Why do you not fight Japan, but instead give the order to fight the Red Army?"

"I am the leader of the Chinese people" Chiang shouted. "I represent the nation. I think my policy is correct . . ."'

Zhang's rebels kept Chiang Kaishek prisoner for the next two weeks. During that time they held long discussions with representatives of the Guomindang and with the Communist Party and the Russian government. In the end they agreed to release Chiang. In return for his freedom, Chiang agreed to form a **United Front** with the Communists against Japan. The Russian government agreed to give them military aid, and Chiang was named Commander-in-Chief of all the Chinese forces.

A United Front

The agreement to form a United Front was made not a moment too soon. The Japanese decided to strike against China before it became too strong and in July 1937, without declaring war, began another invasion of Chinese territory. This time they aimed to conquer the entire country.

Work section

A. Read source A again, then answer these questions:
1. What does the source tell you about the feelings of people in Shanghai towards the Japanese? Quote from the source to illustrate your answer.
2. Explain in your own words what the aim of the anti-Japanese boycott was.
3. How effective, according to this source, was the boycott?

B. Read source B again, then answer these questions:
1. Describe in your own words the demands of the rebels as they appear in this passage.
2. Using the information you have read in this chapter, explain what Chiang Kaishek's policy towards the Japanese was, and why he thought it was correct.
3. Why do you think Chiang asked to be shot? Why do you think Sun did not do so?

C. Study the poster above. How does the picture suggest that Japanese emigrants could have a good life in Manchuria?

THE JAPAN-CHINA WAR, 1937–45

Japanese conquests

In July 1937 Japanese troops provoked local Chinese troops into a fight on the Marco Polo Bridge outside Beijing. Claiming that the Chinese had fired on them, the Japanese launched an attack on army bases around Beijing and then occupied the city itself.

The attack on Beijing had been carefully prepared and was quickly followed by a full-scale invasion of China. Japanese troops swept southwards, pushing back the Guomindang armies everywhere they went. After a three-month siege and heavy aerial bombing, they captured Shanghai, China's most important port, in November 1937. An advance up the Yangzi River led to the capture of Nanjing, the capital, in December. This forced Chiang Kaishek to retreat to Sichuan province where he set up a new, wartime capital in the city of Chongqing.

By the start of 1938 around one million Japanese troops were in China. They had control of all the main cities and lines of communication in the provinces around the mouth of the Yangzi River, China's most fertile and densely-populated area. Later in 1938 they went on to capture the important cities of Wuhan and Guangzhou and occupied the island of Hainan.

For the next five years the Japanese did not make any more advances into China. Japan, a much smaller country than China, simply did not have enough manpower to occupy the whole country. Even in the areas the Japanese occupied they never had total control; for as they went south from Manchuria they had to leave unguarded many of the areas which they had captured. This allowed the Chinese to move back into these areas and take control of the countryside. So from 1938 to 1944 the Japanese occupied the large cities, important railways, airfields, ports and roads, while the countryside stayed mostly in Chinese hands. In the south, the Japanese concentrated on trying to destroy Chiang Kaishek's wartime government in Chongqing, bombing it so hard that it became known as 'the most bombarded city in the world'.

American involvement

By 1941 Japan had around two million men in China – more than half her entire armed forces. But in December 1941 an event occurred to improve the situation facing Chiang Kaishek: the United States of America declared war on Japan after Japan attacked the American naval base at Pearl Harbor in the Pacific Ocean. An immediate result of America's entry into the war was the arrival in Chongqing of American supplies along the Burma Road (see map). Later, American airfields built in south-east China

The Japan-China war, 1937–45

allowed American bombers to smash Japan's sea trade and cut off nearly all her imports.

In April 1944 the Japanese launched a major new offensive in south-east China. Their aim was to destroy the American airfields there. Advancing south from Wuhan, the Japanese captured the city of Changsha and by the end of the year had occupied south-east China, cutting Chiang Kaishek in Chongqing off from the coast. This, however, was the high-water mark of Japanese expansion. In the Pacific Ocean and in Burma, Japanese troops were forced to retreat early in 1945. Then, in the summer of 1945, the war came to a sudden end: on 6 August the Americans used an atomic bomb to destroy Hiroshima, one of the few Japanese cities that had not already been flattened by bombing raids. On 8 August the Russian Red Army declared war on Japan and invaded Manchuria. Finally, on 9 August, a second atomic bomb on the city of Nagasaki persuaded the Japanese government to capitulate. With the surrender of a million Japanese troops in China, the long war between the two countries came to an end.

The people at war

What had the war meant for the ordinary Chinese whose land the Japanese had overrun?

For millions of people it was a war of appalling cruelty. Japanese forces acted with great savagery right from the start of the war. Looting, rape, torture, murder and needless destruction took place in nearly every area they occupied. Aerial bombing of civilians, a new development in warfare, added to the terror. This report by a British journalist in 1938 gives us an idea of what the war meant to the people of Sunkiang, 50 kilometres south of Shanghai:

A. 'Sunkiang . . . presented a scene of indescribable desolation and destruction. Acres of houses have been laid waste as a result of aerial bombing, and there is hardly a building left standing that has not been gutted by fire. Smouldering ruins and deserted streets presented an eerie spectacle, the only living creatures being dogs unnaturally fattened by feasting on corpses. In the whole of Sunkiang, which should contain a densely packed population of approximately 100,000, I saw only five Chinese . . .

No one is able to answer the question of what has happened to the hundreds of thousands, or rather millions, of Chinese who have literally disappeared from this area. The whole thirty-mile route between Shanghai and Sunkiang is like a desert, with rice crops ungathered and left rotting in the fields as far as I could see. The traveller passes a continuous vista of blackened ruins and burnt-out farms guarded over by gruesomely fattened dogs.'

In the eight years of war between China and Japan, some four million Chinese were killed and a further sixty million made homeless.

The Communists at war

One group of Chinese, the Communists, came out of the war stronger than at its start. The Japanese invasion in 1937 and the retreat of Chiang Kaishek to Chongqing gave the Communists many opportunities to expand the area under their control. For, as you have read, the Japanese could not guard all the areas which they conquered as they went south. This meant that the Communists, after waiting for calm to return to such areas, could move in and take control.

Victims of Japanese bombing: Nanjing railway station in November 1937

From 1937 to 1940 Communist fighters gradually moved eastwards from their base at Yanan and took control of many parts of north China. In 1940 they began an offensive called the **Hundred Regiments Battle** in which they attacked Japan's railway communications through north China, paralysing Japanese traffic to and from the south.

To deal with the threat from the Communists the Japanese began an operation in 1941 which they called the **Three All Campaign** – kill all, burn all, destroy all. Their aim was to turn the people against the Communists in areas which supported them, by burning down their villages and crops, slaughtering their animals, poisoning their wells and murdering the peasants. In fact, the Three All Campaign had the opposite effect; it made most peasants hate the Japanese so much that they were more willing than ever before to help the Communists attack them.

In 1945, as the Japanese withdrew from southern China back into Manchuria, the Communists were able to advance into the areas they had left. By 1945 they controlled eighteen such 'liberation areas', most of them in the countryside (see map opposite).

Work section

A. Read source A again, then answer these questions:
1. Describe in your own words the main effects of bombing on the people of Sunkiang.
2. Why do you think nobody was able to answer the question of what had happened to the people of Sunkiang and of the surrounding countryside?
3. What, in your opinion, had happened to them? Explain your answer.
4. Judging by the photograph above, what other effects did aerial bombing have on civilians?

10

THE TWO CHINAS: COMMUNIST AND GUOMINDANG

At the end of the war in 1945, two groups got ready to take back control of China from the defeated Japanese: the Communists in their 'liberation areas' and the Guomindang in Chongqing. Both intended to take control by renewing the civil war between them and fighting for power. What was each side hoping to achieve? What did they have to offer the Chinese people? We can get some answers to these questions by looking at the ways in which they each ran the areas under their control during the war.

Life in Guomindang China

Chiang Kaishek governed his area as a military dictator. Like the Fascist dictators in Europe, Hitler and Mussolini, he believed that a country was best governed by a single supreme leader. He said:

A. 'I believe that unless everyone has absolute trust in one man, we cannot reconstruct the nation and we cannot complete the revolution.'

So, just as Hitler was the 'Fuehrer' of Germany and Mussolini was the 'Duce' of Italy, Chiang Kaishek was called the 'Generalissimo' by his supporters. And while Hitler had an army of 'Brownshirts' and Mussolini an army of 'Blackshirts' to deal with opponents, Chiang Kaishek had a political police force of 'Blueshirts' which specialised in hunting down Communists and in kidnapping, spying and torture.

What was the purpose of Chiang Kaishek's dictatorship? Where was he intending to take China?

First, he aimed to modernise the country. Great efforts were made to unify China by improving the railways, the postal services and telecommunications. Powerful foreign companies such as ICI and Standard Oil were encouraged to build factories in China to help develop its backward industry. A new paper currency was introduced in 1937.

Chiang Kaishek's second aim was to create a sense of national unity among the people. To achieve this he started a **New Life Movement** in 1934. It was based on four ancient ideas – *Li, I, Lien* and *Chih*. His wife explained what this meant in an essay she published in 1934:

B. 'If the national spirit is to be revived, there must be recourse to stable foundations. In the four principles of ancient times we have these foundations. '*Li*' means courtesy; '*I*' means service towards our fellow men and towards ourselves; '*Lien*', honesty and respect for the rights of others; and '*Chih*', high-mindedness and honour.'

The New Life Movement put great stress on public health, self-discipline and honesty. Posters and slogans encouraged people to be clean and hygienic – for example, to blow their noses into handkerchiefs instead of on to the street. The Movement did not, however, try to deal with China's basic welfare problems – lack of medical care, poor housing, ignorance and poverty, so it soon earned a reputation of being trivial.

Another movement started by Chiang Kaishek was the **Rural Service** – a government organisation which sent students into the country during their vacations to help peasants harvest their crops. However, he did nothing to reduce the land taxes which took around half a peasant's income. Nor was he able to prevent a famine in 1929–32 from killing more than three million people. The Rural Service, like the New Life Movement, was criticised as a triviality which did nothing to tackle China's deep-rooted poverty.

Chiang Kaishek and the Guomindang never gained the support of the peasants – who were the majority of the people. The areas where the Guomindang was strongest were the towns and cities of eastern China, where they were supported by bankers, merchants, businessmen and landowners – anybody who stood to benefit from strong government. In the countryside, however, the Guomindang was weak. Few peasants belonged to it, and none of them had any reason to support a government which took their taxes but did little to solve their problems.

A Chinese woodcut showing Guomindang tax collectors seizing the last food and animals from a starving family

Life in the liberation areas

Soon after arriving in Yanan at the end of the Long March, the Communists began making important reforms to the way the land there was owned and farmed. First, big estates of land were confiscated from rich landlords and shared out among peasants who did not have land of their own. Small landlords, however, were allowed to keep their land. Additional help was given to poor peasants in the form of interest-free loans. Rents were reduced and taxes were lightened.

To help peasants improve the way they farmed the land, Red Army engineers made thousands of new farming tools. An agricultural school was set up. 'Saturday Brigades' made up of children, soldiers, and party officials helped peasants work their land at weekends.

The Communists made many social reforms in the 'liberation areas' by abolishing a number of outdated and undesirable practices, particularly in the lives of women. Foot binding – the practice of binding girls' feet tightly in bandages so that they grew up with tiny feet – was abolished. So too was the murder of unwanted babies, child slavery, prostitution and the sale of women. **Women's Associations** were set up to help women free themselves from violent husbands or fathers-in-law.

In Yanan people lived according to the principle of equality. After the town was flattened by Japanese bombing, most of the townspeople moved to caves dug out of the sandstone cliffs above the town. Even the top leaders of the Communist Party lived in the caves and did not have any special luxuries that the ordinary people did not have.

Support for the Communists came mostly from the peasants in the 'liberation areas'. Throughout the war against Japan the Red Army used propaganda to spread Communist ideas in north China. They operated under strict discipline, following Mao Zedong's rules of behaviour (see page 11) and never treating peasants badly. In return, the peasants kept the Red Army informed about Japanese activities, gave them food and shelter, and provided them with recruits.

So, during the war years, China was really two nations in one; a Guomindang China in the coastal towns and cities, and a Communist China in the 'liberation areas' of the countryside.

A Chinese Communist Party poster of 1944 shows peasants helping Red Army soldiers in the war against Japan

---

Work section

A. Test your understanding of this chapter by explaining what the following words and terms mean: Blueshirts; New Life Movement; the Rural Service; 'liberation areas'.

B. Study the woodcut opposite, then answer these questions:
1. What impression does the artist create of the tax collector? Explain how you think the artist managed to create that impression.
2. What do you think were the political views of the artist?
3. Judging by what you have read in this chapter, how fair do you think this portrayal of the Guomindang is? Explain your answer.

C. Study the poster above, then answer these questions:
1. What kinds of help are the peasants giving the soldiers in (a) the top line, (b) the middle line, and (c) the bottom line of the poster?
2. In what other ways are the peasants helping the soldiers?
3. What impression does the artist create of (a) the soldiers, and (b) the peasants?
4. What do you think were the political views of the artist?
5. What do you think were the artist's aims in making this poster?

THE FINAL STRUGGLE, 1945–9

Disunity

As you have read, the Communists and the Guomindang formed a United Front to fight against Japan in 1937. It was, however, a very weak front, for the two sides carried on their civil war with each other at the same time as fighting the war against Japan. In 1938 armed clashes took place between them near Beijing. In 1941 Guomindang forces attacked the Communist New Fourth Army, killing and capturing 10,000 of them. And, throughout the war, Chiang Kaishek used his old tactics of encirclement to surround the Yanan Soviet in yet another extermination campaign, pushing the Communists into an ever-smaller area. So while the Communists were expanding into northern and central China by creating 'liberation areas', they were on the defensive in Yanan.

At the end of the war against Japan in 1945, the Communists and the Guomindang raced for control of the areas that Japan had occupied. The Communists were best placed to win the race, for most Guomindang forces were 1500 kilometres inland, around Chongqing, while the Communists already controlled eighteen 'liberation areas' in the north.

American involvement

The government of the United States of America did not want the Communists to win control of China. To prevent them gaining any more land, the United States Air Force organised a massive airlift, using giant C-54 transport planes, to fly 80,000 of the best Guomindang troops to Nanjing, Shanghai and Beijing. From these key cities, the Guomindang went on to seize most other coastal cities and ports, as well as half the cities in Manchuria.

Although the American government helped the Guomindang with its airlift, it did not want them to renew the civil war. Instead, it wanted the two parties to share power by forming a joint government. So in December 1945 General George C. Marshall, one of America's most respected military leaders, was sent to China to try to bring the two sides together. Marshall did manage to get them round a conference table and to sign a truce, but this broke down early

A street in Shanghai, 1948: desperate savers queue outside a bank to exchange their paper money for gold before inflation makes it worthless

in 1946. The two sides then got ready to fight it out on the battlefield.

The civil war, 1946–9

As the Communists and Guomindang prepared to fight, most people thought the Guomindang would easily win. They had a powerful American-trained and American-equipped army of three million men. They held all the big cities, all the main railway lines, and some of the richest provinces. They had plenty of money and large stocks of weapons. And Chiang Kaishek was recognised by most foreign governments as the true leader of China.

In comparison, the Communists were weak. They held only countryside areas, and not a single big city. They had no air force, few railways, no navy, and an army of one million men. Nor did they have the backing of a foreign country.

The civil war started again in June 1946 when a million Guomindang troops launched a great offensive in north China. By March 1947 they had won a series of battles against the Communists and had even captured Yanan, the Communist capital. However, the Red Army – which was renamed the **People's Liberation Army** (PLA) in 1946 – fought back with great skill. Led by Lin Biao, the PLA avoided major battles with the Guomindang and concentrated on making guerilla attacks against them. This meant making night raids against their bases, blowing up their railway lines, ambushing their patrols, and so on. By using such tactics, the PLA took much of central and northern China during 1947 and forced the Guomindang on to the defensive. And the more land they took, the bigger the PLA became, for thousands of peasants now flocked to join the Communists.

Problems caused by the civil war

Meanwhile, civilians in the Guomindang-held cities were suffering badly. Rapid inflation of the currency was causing great hardship for many of them. As money lost its value and people's wages bought less in the shops, many workers went on strike. Others stopped working and took to robbery instead. As the price of a kilogram of rice rose to half a million Chinese dollars, hungry crowds stormed shops, riots broke out, and public order collapsed. The worse their conditions became, the more the city people

stopped supporting the Guomindang and went over to the Communist Party.

The Blueshirts tried to keep order by using harsh methods against critics of the government. Strict censorship was imposed on the press. Black lists of opponents were drawn up and those named on the lists were systematically murdered. But the Guomindang itself was collapsing as a party. Chiang Kaishek himself admitted in 1947 that the party had become corrupt and disunited:

A. 'To tell the truth, never, in China or abroad, has there been a revolutionary party as decrepit and degenerate as we are today; nor one as lacking spirit, lacking discipline, and even more, lacking standards of right and wrong, as we are today . . . Everyone nourishes the evil habit of caring only for himself.'

The American government, which had given Chiang Kaishek 200 million dollars' worth of aid since 1945, could also see that the Guomindang was a spent force: so in 1947 it cut off all aid to Chiang Kaishek, weakening his position even further.

Communist victory

By 1948 the PLA was large enough to abandon guerilla tactics and to fight the Guomindang head-on. In November 1948 they went on the attack. In large-scale fighting around the towns of Suchow and Yungcheng (see map on page 48), the two sides fought the massive Battle of Huai-Hai (for it was fought between the Huai River and the Lung Hai railway). In the Battle of Huai-Hai the Guomindang lost more than half a million men and huge amounts of equipment. This allowed the PLA to move freely in central China, capturing Beijing in April, Shanghai in May and Guangzhou in October. On 1 October 1949 the Communists were able to proclaim the existence of a new kind of China – the **People's Republic of China**.

The only part of China not under Communist control was the island of Taiwan. For, in January 1949, realising that he had lost the civil war, Chiang Kaishek retreated to the island, taking with him 200,000 Guomindang troops as well as China's gold reserves. From then until his death in 1975, Chiang Kaishek ruled Taiwan as the 'Republic of China', beyond the reach of the Communists.

Work section

A. Using the information you have read in this chapter, make a list of the reasons why the Communists won the civil war of 1946–9.

B. Study source A, then answer these questions:
1. According to Chiang Kaishek, what was wrong with the Guomindang in 1947?
2. Judging by what you have read, what other criticisms could he have made?

C. Make revision notes on what you have read in Chapters 7–11 about China at war. There is a revision guide on the next page to help you organise your notes.

Revision guide

This is an outline of the main points in Chapters 7–11: it is not a complete set of notes that can be copied. You should make your own notes under the headings suggested, if you are unsure how to organise them. They follow on from the notes you have already made on Chapters 1–6.

J. The threat from Japan
1. Japanese expansion, 1895–1915
2. Japan and Manchuria
3. The Manchuria Incident, 1931
4. The occupation of Manchuria, 1931–2

K. Japanese expansion, 1933–7
1. The occupation of China's northern provinces
2. Chinese reactions to Japanese expansion:
   a) the anti-Japanese boycott
   b) the reaction of the Communists
   c) Chiang Kaishek's reactions
3. The Xian Incident, 1936
4. The United Front, 1937

L. The Japan-China War, 1937–45
1. Japanese conquests, 1937–44
2. The effects of the war on the people
3. The growth of the Communist Party during the war

M. The two Chinas
1. Life in the Guomindang areas of China
2. Life in the Communist areas of China

N. The final struggle, 1945–9
1. The race for land in 1945
2. American involvement in China
3. The civil war, 1946–9

Revision exercise

Read the following statements made by Chinese and Japanese people between 1900 and 1949. Then match each statement to the person in the list beneath who was most likely to have made it.

Statement A 'Our best policy lies in taking control of Manchuria. This will enable us to develop our trade, increase our food supply, and get raw materials. Furthermore, our surplus population of 700,000 a year will be taken care of.'

Statement B 'The policy of my party is based on three principles: national freedom from the oppression of foreign countries; democratic government; and a socialist economy. With these three principles we will carry out a National Revolution.'

Statement C 'I do not want a United Front with the Communists. They are no better than bandits. The Japanese are only a disease of the skin. The Communists are a disease of the heart.'

Statement D 'People say that we warlords are cruel and selfish. However, I have to be cruel to be kind. If I do not govern Manchuria with a rod of iron it will fall into the chaos I rescued it from.'

Statement E 'When the news of the Paris Peace Conference finally reached us we were greatly shocked. We at once awoke to the fact that foreign nations were still selfish and militaristic and that they were all great liars. I and a group of friends immediately joined a demonstration against foreign oppression and interference.'

Statement F 'All people, all parties, all armed forces and all classes should unite and wage the war. Only by establishing a national united front can we defeat Japanese imperialism and its running dog, Chiang Kaishek.'

Statement G We practise the I-ho magic boxing so as to protect our country, expel the foreign bandits and kill Christian converts in order to save our people.'

1. A student at Beijing University in May 1919. 2. Chiang Kaishek in 1936.
3. A member of the Japanese government in 1930. 4. A member of the Communist Party in 1935.
5. Sun Yatsen in 1912. 6. A Boxer in 1900. 7. Zhang Zuolin in 1927.

THREE

CHINA UNDER COMMUNIST RULE

Mao Zedong announces the creation of the People's Republic of China on 1 October 1949. Behind him is one of the Deputy Chairmen of the Communist Party, Liu Shaoqi

On 1 October 1949, at the Gate of Heavenly Peace in Tiananmen Square, Beijing, the leaders of the Chinese Communist Party announced to a crowd of 300,000 people that China was now the People's Republic of China. The Chairman of the Party, Mao Zedong, told the excited crowd that the new government would provide China with peace, unity, prosperity and freedom. In short, a revolution in Chinese society, government, law and economy was about to begin.

Mao Zedong had no illusions about what such a revolution might involve. Twenty-two years earlier, in 1927, he had written that:

'A revolution is not the same as inviting people to dinner, or writing an essay, or painting a picture, or doing embroidery; it cannot be so refined, so calm and gentle, or so mild, courteous, restrained and magnanimous. A revolution is an act of violence by which one class overthrows another.'

Part Three of this book shows how China was transformed by a massive revolution in the years after 1949, and how this revolution involved many acts of violence. Let us begin by finding out what the new government hoped to achieve.

12

THE COMMUNIST STATE

The intentions of the Communists

Two days before they proclaimed the People's Republic of China, the Communist Party leaders held a conference to decide their future policy. On 29 September 1949 the Conference drew up a **Common Programme** outlining the Party's aims and intentions for the future.

The Common Programme began by explaining that the new government of China would be a 'People's Democratic Dictatorship.' This meant that the government would be a democracy for most people but a dictatorship for 'reactionaries' – with anybody opposed to the Communists being classed as a reactionary.

The Common Programme went on to state that:

A. 'The People's Republic of China strives for independence, democracy, peace, unity, prosperity, and the strength of China . . . It must systematically transform . . . the land ownership system into a system of peasant land ownership . . . It must steadily transform the country from an agricultural into an industrial one . . . The people shall have freedom of thought, speech, publication, assembly, religious belief and the freedom of holding processions and demonstrations. The People's Republic of China shall abolish the feudal system which holds women in bondage. Women shall enjoy equal rights with men . . . All nationalities in the People's Republic shall have equal rights and duties . . .

The People's Republic of China shall suppress all counter-revolutionary activities, severely punish all Guomindang counter-revolutionary war criminals and other leading counter-revolutionary elements . . . Feudal landlords, capitalists and reactionary elements in general shall be deprived of their political rights.

The People's Republic shall unite with all peace-loving and freedom-loving countries and people throughout the world, first of all with the USSR, all People's Democracies, and all oppressed nations.'

Problems facing the Communists

It was one thing to have good intentions, but quite another to put them into practice. All sorts of problems stood in the way.

For a start, agricultural output had dropped drastically: three years of civil war had taken millions

'New Year's Thanks to the Army.' A Chinese poster of 1950 showing happy relations between peasants and the People's Liberation Army

of peasants away from their fields and had destroyed countless dams, irrigation systems, canals and roads. All this reduced the amount of food that could be grown and marketed. And yet the population was growing by around 15 million a year, so there were more mouths to feed than ever before.

In the cities, the disruption of the civil war had brought chaos to the transport, telecommunications and energy systems. Runaway inflation had made the currency worthless. There was a high level of unemployment. Many public officials had grown used to bribery and corruption under Chiang Kaishek's rule, so local government was often slow and inefficient.

Then there was the threat that Chiang Kaishek, with 200,000 troops and much of China's foreign currency and gold reserves in Taiwan, would try to stage a come-back by invading mainland China.

Above all, the greatest problem was the one that, over the past fifty years, had defeated the Manchu dynasty, Sun Yatsen and Yuan Shikai, the warlords and the Guomindang: the problem of holding China together as a single, united country.

The government of Communist China

The first action of the Communists after seizing power was to reorganise the government of China. They began by grouping the country's eighteen provinces into six regions. In each region they set up a series of councils to run each subdivision of the region, from the provinces down to counties, cities, districts and towns. At each of these levels there was also a Communist Party committee which made sure that the councils put Communist policies into effect.

The Party itself was run on the principle of Democratic Centralism, which means that Party members have to obey strict discipline and give total obedience to the Party leaders. The leaders themselves took over all the most important positions in the government. Chairman Mao Zedong, for example, became Head of State, while Zhou Enlai became Prime Minister as well as Foreign Minister.

The People's Liberation Army – the five million soldiers who had won the civil war – had an important role to play in the new system of government. The commanders of the PLA shared all the tasks of government with the councils that ran the six regions into which China had been divided. PLA troops were used in many areas to tackle urgent problems, such as rebuilding railway lines, bridges and ports. In the outlying regions of Xinjiang, Tibet and Inner Mongolia, PLA troops were used as Production and Construction Armies, helping not only to build up their backward economies but also to bring them under firmer control than any Chinese government had managed in the past hundred years.

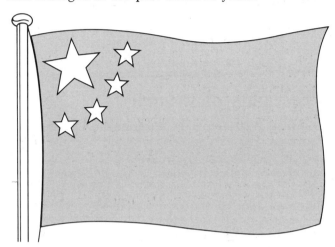

The new flag of China in 1949: five gold stars on a red background. The large star stands for the Common Programme of the Party. The four smaller stars represent the workers, peasants, the lower middle class and 'patriotic' capitalists

Work section

A. Test your understanding of this chapter by explaining what these terms mean: democracy; dictatorship; reactionaries; democratic centralism.

B. Study source A, then describe how you think each of the following might have reacted to the Common Programme of the Communist Party. Quote from the source to illustrate your answer in each case.

1 A wealthy landlord.
2 A young woman.
3 A landless peasant.
4 A Buddhist monk.
5 A factory worker.

6 A member of the Guomindang.
7 A Tibetan nomad.
8 A land-owning peasant.
9 A Shanghai banker.
10 A member of the American government.

C. Study the poster on the opposite page, then answer these questions:
1. Suggest why, in 1950, peasants might want to give 'New Year's Thanks to the Army'.
2. In what ways are the peasants showing their thanks?
3. What do you think was the aim of the artist in painting this poster?
4. How might an opponent of the Communist Party have painted a different scene in early 1950?

D. Turn back to page 6 and compare the flag of Republican China on that page with the Communist flag on this page. Read the information about each flag, and then answer these questions:
1. In what ways does the Communist flag differ from the Republican flag?
2. What similarity is there between the two flags?
3. Why do you think the Communists introduced this new flag in 1949?

YEARS OF GREAT CHANGE, 1950–3

The first three years of the People's Republic of China were a time of great change that affected virtually all Chinese people. The first great change affected the rights of the 270 million females who made up half the population.

The rights of women

In April 1950 the new government introduced a **Marriage Law**. This ended some of the worst features of a woman's life. Arranged marriages, the marriage of children, the killing of unwanted girl babies, and bigamy were all made illegal. The minimum age for marriage was fixed at twenty for men and eighteen for women. Husbands and wives now jointly owned the family property, where before it had belonged to the husband only. Divorce by mutual consent was introduced. And a further law in February 1951 gave expectant mothers maternity benefit of full wages for two months after the birth of the child.

Land reform

The next great area of reform which the new government tackled was the system of land ownership. As you have read (page 23) the Communists had already started to divide land among the peasants in Yanan. They did the same in the 'liberation areas' which came under their control during the civil war. So, by 1949, the process of giving land to landless peasants was already under way in many parts of the country.

On 30 June 1950 an **Agrarian Reform Law** speeded up the process of land reform. Communist Party members went into the countryside to teach poor peasants how to work out the social class of everyone in their community. The aim was to decide whether people were landlords, 'rich' peasants (meaning those who hired other peasants to work for them), 'middle' or 'poor' peasants. 'Poor' peasants were then encouraged to hold mass meetings in which they could 'speak bitterness' about their poverty and denounce those landlords who had treated them badly in the past.

Once every villager's social class had been decided, land was taken from those who had more than they needed for their own use, and given to those who had none. Between 1950 and 1952 some 47 million hectares (about 40 per cent of all cultivated land) were taken away from landlords and 'rich' peasants, and given to around 300 million peasants.

As time went by, the 'speak bitterness' meetings became very bitter indeed, and the land reform was

A Chinese poster of 1950 showing a 'speak bitterness' meeting at which peasants denounce their landlord

carried out with increasing violence. The 'speak bitterness' meetings often ended with the execution of landlords who had been particularly cruel to their tenants. Nobody knows exactly how many were killed, but the figure is probably between 2 and 4 million.

The Agrarian Reform Law of 1950 did not live up to every peasant's expectations. After receiving their land, peasants were often bitterly disappointed when they realised they had no equipment to cultivate it, nor the money to buy equipment. Many of them therefore joined **mutual aid teams** of around ten households which worked together on the land, sharing their animals and their equipment.

The economy

The new government took rapid steps to overcome China's grave economic problems. To start with, all major banks, the railway network, and about a third of heavy industry were taken away from their owners and made into state property. The profits from these enterprises were then paid direct into the State Treasury, giving the government around two thirds of its yearly income.

A People's Bank was opened in 1951 to replace the private banks. The People's Bank had control of all financial transactions as well as of the issue of money. It was therefore able to get rid of inflation entirely by the mid-1950s.

To overcome the threat of a food shortage, farmers had to sell 15 to 20 per cent of their grain to the government at a fixed low price. They also had to pay

A People's Court in 1953. The man on the stool is on trial for attempting to sell one of his family. She is sitting on the other stool with a white cloth over her head. The man squatting by the judges' table is repeating the evidence in a loud voice for the crowd to hear. The sale of women was common in China before the 1950 Marriage Law

an Agricultural Tax on their produce. The tax was efficiently collected by the Party members who toured the villages, helping poor peasants to put the Agrarian Reform Law into effect.

The organisation of the people

The Communist Party put a great deal of effort into strengthening its position and getting rid of those whom it called 'reactionaries'.

During 1950 and 1951 the Party organised mass rallies at which public 'enemies' and counter-revolutionaries were publicly tried. Most of the accused were people who had collaborated with the Japanese, or who had fought in the Guomindang armies. Eventually, around a million of these 'reactionaries' were executed.

In 1951 the Party began a movement for '**thought reform**'. It was called the 'Movement for the Study of Mao Zedong's Thought' and involved close study of his writings combined with public self-criticism at Party meetings.

To concentrate the people's attention on specific problems, the Party organised **mass campaigns**. A 'Three Antis Campaign' was launched in 1951 against

corruption, waste and too much 'red tape'. In 1952 the 'Five Antis Campaign' aimed to get rid of bribery, tax evasion, fraud, theft of government property, and spying. People found guilty of these offences were sent to labour camps to be 're-educated' with thought reform.

And to strengthen the Party itself, every sector of the population – peasants, factory workers, young people, women, students, and so on – was encouraged to join Party-run interest groups. Groups such as the Women's League for Democracy, the Young Pioneers and the China-Russia Friendship Association quickly sprang up all over China.

Because the Party controlled these organisations, it was easily able to use the members for its own purposes – for example, by involving them in mass rallies in Beijing's Tienanmen Square. A remarkable example of the Party's ability to organise the Chinese people was the 'Swat the Fly' campaign: throughout the 1950s every citizen was asked to kill at least ten flies each per day. With a population of nearly 600 million, this meant the death of trillions of flies, resulting in their virtual extinction in some parts of the country.

Work section

A. Test your understanding of this chapter by explaining what the following terms mean: Agrarian Reform Law; 'speak bitterness' meetings; mutual aid teams; 'thought reform'; mass campaigns.

B. During the first year after the Marriage Law was passed, more than a million married couples obtained divorces. Bearing in mind that there were some 70 million married couples, does this suggest that the Marriage Law was badly needed? Explain your answer.

C. Study the poster opposite, then answer these questions:
   1. What impression does the artist create of (a) the landlord, and (b) the peasants?
   2. How does the poster show that the Agrarian Reform Law was carried out with the encouragement of the Communist Party?
   3. What, in your opinion, is the point of this poster? Explain your answer.

14

A FIVE-YEAR PLAN AND A HUNDRED FLOWERS, 1953–7

Mao Zedong said in 1949, shortly after coming to power:

A. 'Of all the things in the world, people are the most precious. Under the leadership of the Communist Party, as long as there are people, every kind of miracle can be performed.'

Some miracles, however, need money as well as people; so one of Mao Zedong's first actions after taking power was to ask the USSR, China's Communist neighbour, for financial help. In December 1949 he travelled to Moscow for talks with Joseph Stalin, the Soviet leader.

One result of the talks between Mao and Stalin was a **Treaty of Friendship, Alliance and Mutual Assistance** which provided China with financial aid and technical advice. It was, however, 'like getting meat out of the mouth of a tiger', Mao said when he returned: the aid amounted to only $300 million over the next five years, most of it in the form of credits rather than cash. More valuably, perhaps, the Treaty provided 10,000 engineers and planning experts to help develop China's economy.

The first Five-Year Plan

Under the influence of their Russian advisers, the Chinese drew up a Five-Year Plan for the development of their economy. The Plan, which ran from 1953 to 1957, gave priority to heavy industry – steel, coal, machinery and the like – the centre-piece being nearly 700 new production plants in central China and Manchuria. The photograph below gives an idea of the large scale of these new plants. In contrast, China's light industry – such as cotton-making and food processing – was neglected in favour of heavy industry, so the people had to put up with only a slow growth in their living standards and in the availability of consumer goods.

The achievements of the first Five-Year Plan can be judged from this table of figures:

The first Five-Year Plan, 1953–7
Output in millions of tonnes

	1952	1957 (planned)	1957 (actual output)
Coal	63.5	113.0	124.0
Pig-iron	1.9	4.7	5.8
Steel	1.3	4.1	5.2
Oil	0.4	2.0	1.4
Cement	2.6	6.0	4.6
Chemical fertiliser	0.2	0.6	0.7

An expanding industry meant an expanding number of workers in the towns and cities. And that, of course, meant more mouths to feed. So the Five-Year Plan also aimed to increase the output of food from China's farms by turning them into cooperatives.

The steelworks at Anshan, Manchuria, built in the 1950s as part of the first Five-Year Plan.

The cooperative farms

As you have read, the Agrarian Reform Law of 1950 gave land to about 300 million peasants. Around half of them were able to farm their land by themselves. The others, whose fields were too small or who did not own farming tools, worked together in mutual-aid teams, sharing their equipment and their animals.

The government, however, did not want to leave land reform at that stage. For a start, most peasants' farms were too small to be farmed efficiently, meaning that they could not increase food output to the level needed for the Five-Year Plan. Second, the government feared that if the peasants kept their plots of land, they would become a new class in society, concerned only to make profits for themselves and opposed to any change in their position.

So, from 1953, the government and the Party made great efforts to persuade peasants to join what they called **lower-stage cooperatives**. This meant that thirty to fifty families, usually the people of one village, pooled their land and their labour to make one bigger, more efficient farm. Although the families still legally owned their plots of land, the land was actually on permanent loan to the cooperative, which paid each family a rent for its use.

The Five-Year Plan went much further than this – by joining the lower-stage cooperatives into much bigger **higher-stage cooperatives**. These consisted of 200 to 300 families, usually the people of a group of villages. The big difference between these and the lower-stage cooperatives was that the families were not paid rent for the use of their land. They received only wages for their labour. They had to surrender the title deeds to their land, their equipment and their animals to the cooperative. They were allowed to keep only a few square metres for their personal use – for growing vegetables or raising chickens, for example.

By the end of 1956, 95 out of every 100 peasant families had joined higher-stage cooperatives. Most of the 300 million peasants who had received land in 1950 were therefore landless again.

The Hundred Flowers

The Five-Year Plan put Chinese society under a terrific strain. The city population rose by around 40 million, causing overcrowding, food shortages and housing problems, while many peasants found plenty to complain about in the new higher-stage cooperatives. The Communist Party was losing some of its early popularity, and many people had harsh words to say about its leaders.

Mao Zedong decided in 1956 to allow the people to let off steam by saying what they wanted about the Communist Party, its policies and its leaders. He said in a speech that 'It is only by using discussion, criticism and reasoning that we can really foster correct ideas, overcome wrong ideas and really settle issues'. Putting it another way, he quoted from ancient Chinese history, saying 'Let a hundred flowers bloom', meaning that free speech and argument were healthy and should be encouraged.

For a while, Chinese people said exactly what they liked. But often they spoke more freely than Mao Zedong liked. This statement by a former warlord, Chen Mingshu, shows the sort of thing people were thinking and saying in 1956–7.

B. 'Mao is hot-tempered and not sober-minded; impetuous and not prudent; reckless and not self-assured; incisive and not thoughtful. He loves to be great and meritorious [*deserving praise*] but needs to become more observant of the facts in order to learn the truth. He places confidence in false reports and meets only those who seek to please him.'

In June 1957 Mao Zedong suddenly cracked down on his critics. Many were arrested and sent off to camps in the countryside for 'thought reform'. Others were sacked from their jobs. People were forbidden to speak freely and the press was censored. The 'Hundred Flowers' withered as rapidly as they had bloomed.

Work section

A. Test your understanding of this chapter by explaining what the following terms mean: Five-Year Plan; cooperative farm; lower-stage cooperative; higher-stage cooperative; 'let a hundred flowers bloom'.

B. Study the table of output for the first Five-Year Plan opposite. Judging by these figures, how successful was the Plan? Quote figures from the table to support your answer.

C. Read source B again. Judging by what you have read in this and the previous chapter, what aspects of Communist rule do you think led Chen Mingshu to make these criticisms of Mao Zedong?

D. Divide a page into two columns. In one column list the advantages of big cooperative farms over small, privately owned farms. In the other column, list their disadvantages from a peasant's point of view. Do you think the advantages outweigh the disadvantages, or vice versa? Explain your answer.

THE GREAT LEAP FORWARD, 1958

In the summer of 1958 Mao Zedong made a tour of the Chinese countryside. On his return to Beijing he said:

A. 'During this trip I have witnessed the tremendous energy of the masses. On this foundation it is possible to accomplish any task whatsoever.'

The task he had in mind was to make China into one of the world's leading industrial nations at the same time as improving her agriculture. This would be done through a second Five-Year Plan, running from 1958 to 1963. Mao intended that the Chinese economy would overtake that of Britain within fifteen years and that of America in twenty to thirty years. He called the plan the '**Great Leap Forward**'.

The communes

Unlike the first Five-Year Plan, the Great Leap Forward aimed to develop agriculture as well as industry, both heavy and light, all at the same time. The key to achieving this was the reorganisation of the Chinese people into **communes**.

Communes were groups of villages which varied in size from a few square kilometres to that of a British county. The average commune contained about 5000 families who gave up their land, their animals and their equipment to common ownership by all members of the commune.

The purpose of the communes was to release what Mao called 'the tremendous energy of the masses' by making sure that time and effort were not wasted and that the members of a commune could work at a great variety of tasks. Mao said:

B. 'The advantage of People's Communes lies in the fact that they combine industry, agriculture, commerce, education and military affairs.'

At first, the communes were organised so that nothing could distract people from their work. Around four million communal eating halls were set up so that the number of people who spent time cooking meals was reduced. Several million children were put into nurseries and schools so that both parents in a family were freed for full-time work. Old and infirm people were moved into 'houses of happiness' so that their families did not have to take time off work to look after them.

Communes controlled almost every activity in a person's life because they combined several different functions. First, a commune was a unit of local

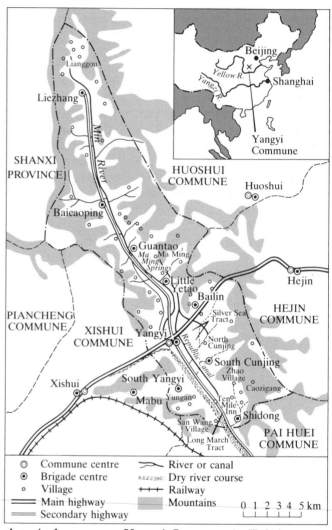

A typical commune: Yangyi Commune in Hebei province, set up in 1958

government, with a committee made up of peasants, Party members and soldiers running schools, clinics, nurseries, eating halls, entertainments and other public services. Second, a commune was a unit of work organisation, with the work of the commune divided among work teams of a dozen families, and grouped into work brigades of a dozen work teams. And thirdly, the commune was a unit of the Communist Party, with a Party committee making sure that the commune always followed Party decisions.

The speed with which communes were created astounded not only the Chinese but the rest of the world too. By the end of 1958 about 700 million people (roughly 90 per cent of the population) had been placed into 26,578 communes in all parts of the country.

Members of a commune helping to build a new canal in 1958

Propaganda and enthusiasm

A key element in the Great Leap Forward was Party propaganda. The Party and the government made every effort to whip the people into a frenzy of enthusiasm for their work. Posters, slogans and newspaper articles urged the Chinese to work long hours, whatever the weather and no matter how bad the conditions. Wherever people worked, loudspeakers played revolutionary music and stirring speeches, encouraging workers not only to reach but to exceed the Plan's targets.

As a result, many impressive construction projects were completed in record time. Hugo Portisch, a European journalist, later described in his book *Eyewitness in China* how a gigantic dam was built near Beijing:

C. 'There were not enough machines, there was no cement, no mortar and other building materials. Beijingers were summoned to build this dam with their bare hands and feet by voluntary shift work. Hundreds of thousands of inhabitants of Beijing, including all the civil servants and university professors, doctors, students, etc. set out to execute the order. In eight-hour shifts they worked day and night without a break. They scratched away the earth from the surrounding hills often with no more than their fingernails, they split stones with the most primitive tools, and carried earth and stone in little baskets on carrying poles to the river bed, where more thousands stood and stamped the stones and earth flat with their feet, urged on by Party . . . men with megaphones . . . Mao Zedong himself and all the members of the Politburo and the government came and joined in the work of building the dam . . . In six months the dam was built. It is 2088 feet high and 38.2 feet wide at its base.'

The backyard steel campaign

Communes were expected to contribute to the Great Leap Forward in small as well as big projects. Small commune factories were set up to make all kinds of industrial products such as cement, ball bearings and chemical fertiliser. Particular emphasis was placed on the making of steel, so 600,000 'backyard steel furnaces' were set up in towns and villages all over China. Before long, these little furnaces, each one capable making only a few tonnes of steel, had turned out 11 million tonnes of steel – 65 per cent more than the total for 1957.

As 1958 wore on, the figures for the production of steel, coal, timber, cement, fertiliser, and a hundred other industrial products showed a spectacular rise. In agriculture there were record harvests of cotton and grain. It began to seem that Mao Zedong was right – that it really was 'possible to accomplish any task whatsoever'.

Work section

A. Test your understanding of this chapter by explaining what the following terms mean: Great Leap Forward; commune; work team; work brigade; backyard steel.

B. Study source C, then answer these questions:
  1. a) According to Hugo Portisch, what difficulties were involved in making the dam?
     b) How were these difficulties overcome?
  2. a) How does Hugo Portisch suggest that people worked on the dam against their will?
     b) How does he suggest that many people felt real enthusiasm for their work?

C. Study the photograph above, then answer these questions:
  1. Suggest why the workers in the foreground appear to be enjoying their work.
  2. Does the photograph help to confirm or disprove any of the evidence in source C? Explain your answer.

16

'THREE BITTER YEARS': THE CRISIS OF 1959–61

'Chaos on a grand scale'

Only months after Mao Zedong launched the Great Leap Forward, things began to go dreadfully wrong. This extract from an interview between a British journalist and the manager of a chemical factory gives us an idea of what was happening:

A. 'Ours is the only chemical factory of its kind and the boiler is seventy years old. But one day a Party official arrived and told me to increase the pressure in the boiler from a hundred to a hundred and fifty pounds per square inch so that the reactor process could be completed nine times a day instead of six. When I told him he was turning it into a bomb, he accused me of being a bourgeois [*middle class*] reactionary. So what was I to do? Great Leap? The connecting pipe burst when the pressure reached a hundred and twenty pounds, and we were out of production for a week while repairs were made.'

Scenes like that were repeated all over China in 1958–9. Everywhere, Party workers urged people to produce more and to produce it faster. As a result, old and overworked machines fell apart under the strain. Factory workers fell asleep at their benches and suffered accidents through carelessness brought on by exhaustion.

It wasn't only in the factories that the Great Leap failed to take off. The 'backyard steel' campaign also failed. Three million of the eleven million tonnes of steel made in backyard furnaces were too impure for industrial use and had to be thrown away as scrap. But worse was to come. So many furnaces were built that, eventually, one person in ten was employed in making steel. This took people away from the fields, reducing the amount of food that could be grown. The furnaces also used so much of the country's coal supplies that railway locomotives had no fuel to run on. And so much extra steel was made that there were not enough railway trains to take it to the industrial centres where it was needed.

Mao Zedong admitted in 1959 that the Great Leap Forward had failed. In a speech to the Party leaders, he said:

B. 'Coal and iron cannot walk by themselves. They need vehicles to transport them. This I did not foresee. I and the Premier did not concern ourselves with this point. You could say we were ignorant of it . . . I am a complete outsider when it comes to economic construction. I understand nothing about industrial planning. Comrades, in 1958 and 1959, the main responsibility was mine, and you should take me to task . . . The chaos caused was on a grand scale, and I take responsibility. Comrades, you must all analyse your own responsibility . . . If you have to fart, fart! You will feel much better for it.'

The farming crisis

The Great Leap Forward failed as badly in the countryside as it did in the towns. Although the weather in 1958 was excellent, two problems prevented the harvest from being a good one. First, so many peasants were working in industry, especially in backyard steel-making, that there were too few people to harvest the crops properly. Second, Party officials ignored this fact and falsely claimed that the grain harvest had been a record 260 million tonnes. As a result, many communal eating halls started giving the peasants very generous meals, using up valuable food stocks.

None of this would have mattered if the next year's harvest had been good. But the weather in 1959 was very bad. In some parts of China there were floods, in other parts there was drought. The result was a harvest of only 170 million tonnes. Before long, people were going hungry. Some began to starve.

To complete the farming crisis, the weather in 1960 was even worse than in 1959. The bad weather, combined with the chaos caused by the Great Leap Forward, reduced the harvest to 144 million tonnes. This led to a major famine, killing around 9 million people in 1960 alone. The government introduced a rationing system under which most people were given a maximum of 125 grams of grain a day, but the death toll continued to rise. Between 1959 and 1962 some 20 million Chinese died of starvation and related diseases.

The rise of the moderates

The 'three bitter years', as the Chinese called the famine years of 1959–61, were partly the result of Mao Zedong's Great Leap Forward policies. As Liu Shaoqi, a deputy leader of the Party, put it:

C. 'The disaster was seventy per cent man-made and thirty per cent due to natural causes.'

Not unnaturally, some Party leaders blamed Mao personally for what had happened, and demanded his

'Huhsien County's New Look.' A painting by Tung Chengyi, a peasant, of the commune where he lived

resignation. However, Mao was too popular among the masses of Chinese people for them to get rid of him easily. So the Party leaders simply persuaded him to hand over the post of Head of State to Liu Shaoqi, leaving him with only one post, that of Party Chairman. This meant that Mao was no longer involved in the routine, practical work of governing China. That was now done by a group of more moderate leaders – Head of State Liu Shaoqi, Prime Minister Zhou Enlai and Party Secretary Deng Xiaoping.

Now that they controlled the government, the moderates introduced more realistic economic policies. Late in 1960 they abandoned the Great Leap Forward. Communes were reduced in size to make them more manageable. Peasants working in back-yard steel production were sent back to the fields. Peasants were allowed their own private plots again, and to sell part of what they grew at market for their own profit. Town workers' wages were increased.

Although the moderates now ran the economy, this did not mean that Mao Zedong had lost his grip. Mao was still regarded by most Chinese as a great revolutionary hero. And although the moderates did not allow him a say in running the economy, he continued to have great influence over the mass of the people. He used this influence in 1966 to get rid of the moderates by starting a new political revolution that would soon be known throughout the world as the **Cultural Revolution**.

Work section

A. Read source A again, then answer these questions:
1. Why did the Party official tell the manager to increase the pressure in the boiler?
2. Why do you think the manager did so even though he thought the boiler would explode?
3. Why do you think the Party official ignored the manager's advice that he was 'turning it into a bomb'?

B. Read source C again, then answer these questions:
1. What was the disaster that Liu Shaoqi was referring to?
2. Judging by what you have read in this and the previous chapter, list the causes of the disaster which you think were a) 'man-made', and b) 'natural'.
3. How far does source B support the view expressed in source C?
4. In the light of your answer to the last question, do you agree or disagree with Liu Shaoqi's opinion? Explain your answer.

C. Study the painting above, then answer these questions:
1. What impression does the artist give of his commune?
2. How useful do you find this painting as a source of evidence about Chinese communes? Explain your answer.

17

THE CULTURAL REVOLUTION, 1966–9

Which road to follow?

From 1962 to 1966 the leaders of the Communist Party argued with one another about which road they should follow in developing China.

The moderates, led by Liu Shaoqi and Deng Xiaoping, wanted to introduce more incentives to get the peasants in the communes working hard. They wanted, for example, to let the peasants have larger private plots and to pay them wages according to how much work they did. They also believed in going back to the ideas of the first Five-Year Plan to build up industry on Russian lines. And to manage industry more efficiently, they wanted to create a new class of skilled managers.

Mao Zedong totally opposed the policies of the moderates. He said they were taking the 'capitalist road' and that they were allowing people to forget the original aims of the Communist Party. In 1962 he launched a **Socialist Education Movement** to get people back on the right road to Communism. He also launched a 'four clean-ups campaign' to get rid of corruption and bad management in the Party and to discourage people who showed signs of 'capitalist' behaviour – for example, peasants who spent more time on their private plots than on the communal land.

Beijing, 1967. Red Guards parade a government official through the streets in a dunce's hat to show that he had been involved in an anti-revolutionary group

Support for Mao

From 1962 to 1966 Mao continually urged the Party to keep in touch with the ordinary people of China and to avoid the 'capitalist road'. For much of the time his advice fell on deaf ears. But in 1965 he gained powerful support from Lin Biao, the Minister of Defence. In that year, Lin Biao abolished all ranks in the People's Liberation Army, thus making all soldiers equal. Every soldier was given a copy of a newly published book, 'Quotations from Chairman Mao Zedong', known from its size and cover as '**The Little Red Book**', and were ordered to study it. So although nobody in the government supported his ideas, Mao now had the support of the four million strong People's Liberation Army.

With the backing of Lin Biao and the PLA, Mao was strong enough to launch a new super-campaign against 'capitalists' and any other 'reactionaries' who stood in the way of true Communism. The campaign began in 1966 and was known as 'The Great Proletarian Cultural Revolution'.

The Red Guards

The Cultural Revolution began among schoolchildren and students in Beijing. In the summer of 1966 students in Beijing formed into military groups which they called **Red Guards**. At the same time, schools and colleges were shut down for six months so that the curriculum could be rewritten to make young people more aware of Communist ideas. This meant that the Red Guards had plenty of time to give to political activities. Their first aim was to get rid of all 'capitalist' and 'bourgeois' influences in schools and colleges.

The Red Guards began with a 'Four Olds' campaign against old ideas, old culture, old customs and old habits. They expressed their criticisms in hundreds of thousands of wall posters like the one in the photograph opposite. They marched through Beijing in monster parades numbering over a million at a time. And they attacked anything which seemed to them 'capitalist' or 'bourgeois'.

Before long, the Red Guards were using violence to achieve their aims. They shaved off the hair of girls with Western hairstyles and ripped off Western-style clothes. They smashed the windows of shops selling cosmetics, pets, jazz records, chess sets, fur coats, and a thousand other 'bourgeois' luxuries. They burnt down bookshops and libraries, and closed museums and art galleries, churches, temples and theatres. They forbade couples to hold hands in

A monster rally of 700,000 Red Guards in Tienanmen Square in Beijing in 1966

public. They renamed places which had 'reactionary' names, so that the Square of Heavenly Peace where they held their parades became 'East Wind Square' and Beijing itself became 'The East is Red'.

Mao Zedong encouraged all these activities, saying that 'To rebel is justified'. The Red Guards were given every help in their campaign: they were, for example, given the right to travel free on the Chinese railways so that they could visit places connected with the Long March or take part in monster rallies in Beijing. The police were under orders not to oppose them and the PLA often gave them enthusiastic support.

As a result, the Red Guards ran wild. By 1967 law and order had broken down in many parts of China. For much of 1967 the country was in a state of virtual civil war as Red Guards fought against 'reactionaries' and then, as they argued amongst themselves, with each other. In all, it is thought that they killed around 400,000 people. Countless thousands more were beaten up, humiliated, tortured and imprisoned.

The cult of Mao Zedong

Throughout the Cultural Revolution the Red Guards followed every word of Mao Zedong. Much of their time was spent reading and memorising the Little Red Book, 740 million copies of which were printed between 1966 and 1969. Pictures, busts and statues of Mao were put up in every street and workplace. Many people bowed before his picture after getting up in the morning and before getting into bed at night. Just as much as they worshipped Mao, they hated Liu Shaoqi and Deng Xiaoping, the leading moderates in the government. Both were expelled from the Party and Liu was imprisoned, dying in captivity in 1969.

In September 1967 Mao Zedong attempted to restore order to China. Schools and colleges were reopened and he called on young people to return to their studies. In areas where the Red Guards were using violence, the PLA stepped in to disarm and disband them. To get rid of the millions of Red Guards who now occupied the cities, Mao encouraged them to 'go down to the country' to re-educate themselves by learning from the peasants. In all, some 18 million young people went down to the country. And to restore order in areas where government had broken down, the PLA set up Revolutionary Committees consisting of peasants, soldiers and Red Guards.

By 1969 order had been restored in most areas and the Cultural Revolution was over. The cost to China had been high. Young people had missed so much of their education that, by 1981, the government estimated that around 120 million people under the age of 45 could not read or write. Industrial output fell drastically. Farming was severely disrupted. For the second time in ten years, China had suffered 'chaos on a grand scale' under Mao Zedong's leadership.

Work section

A. Test your understanding of this chapter by explaining what the following terms mean: the 'capitalist road'; the Little Red Book; the Cultural Revolution; 'going down to the country'.

B. Look at the photograph opposite. Using your imagination as well as the information in this chapter, suggest what the government official had done to be treated in this way.

C. Write a wall poster (in English) of about fifty words criticising 'capitalist' influences in your school and saying what actions you want your fellow students to take.

18

POWER STRUGGLES, 1969–76

Four key figures in the struggle for power; from right to left, Mao Zedong in Red Guard uniform, Lin Biao speaking to Red Guards, Zhou Enlai and Jiang Qing at a rally in Beijing in 1969

When Mao Zedong announced in 1969 that the Cultural Revolution was over, he was in a very strong political position. Most of the moderates had been expelled from the Party and from the government, leaving his own supporters in all the top positions.

'Project 571'

Mao's position was not entirely secure, however. Lin Biao, the Defence Minister and head of the PLA, who had supported Mao throughout the Cultural Revolution, began to doubt whether he could continue supporting him.

On the surface it seemed that the two men were very close. A Party conference in 1969 named Lin as Mao's second-in-command, and described him as 'closest comrade-in-arms and successor to Mao Zedong'. But, behind the scenes, the two men mistrusted each other. Mao feared that Lin would not wait until he was dead before trying to take his post as Chairman; while Lin was convinced that Mao was power-mad and unwilling to share any of his authority. In a secret document, he wrote:

> 'B. 52 [*his code-name for Mao*] is a paranoid and a sadist . . . the greatest dictator and tyrant in China's history.'

To weaken Lin's position, Mao got rid of several Party leaders who supported him. Realising what was happening, Lin plotted to overthrow Mao. In 1971 he drew up a plan which he code-named 'Project 571' to assassinate Mao and take power as Chairman himself. The plot was discovered, however, and Lin and his fellow plotters fled. They tried to escape from China by air, but were all killed when their aircraft crashed in a desert in Mongolia.

Right versus left

Following the death of Lin Biao, the old arguments began again about which road the government should follow in developing China. In 1973, elections to the Politburo (the Party's ruling body) produced a split between right-wing moderates and left-wing radicals.

The Right was led by the Prime Minister, Zhou Enlai, and the Deputy Prime Minister, Deng Xiaoping. Deng, as you have read, had been expelled from the Party during the Cultural Revolution, but was brought back to power in the 1973 elections. Zhou and Deng were supported by the Party and the PLA.

The Left was led by Mao's wife, Jiang Qing, and three radical politicians from Shanghai. Known as the **Gang of Four**, they were supported by the trade unions, by the Communist Youth League and by the militias of the big cities. They had a big advantage over the Right because they had control of the press and the radio.

What divided the Right from the Left? They disagreed over nearly everything, but the basic difference between them was about whether politics was more important than the Chinese economy. The Right wanted an end to the political arguments and struggles that had dominated Chinese life since 1966. Instead, they wanted the Party and government to put all their efforts into building up a strong and wealthy China.

The Left, on the other hand, wanted to continue the political struggle. For them, the struggle between social classes was the most important thing in life. Capitalists and reactionaries of all kinds must be weeded out, they believed. China must follow the 'mass line' – that is, serving the people and giving them a full share in decision-making. Close study of Mao Zedong's thoughts was the key to understanding the struggle, they said.

The rise and fall of the Gang of Four

Between 1974 and 1976 the Left and the Right struggled fiercely for power. The Right backed a plan for **Four Modernisations** which Zhou Enlai put forward

Tienanmen Square, Beijing, April 1976, shortly before police removed wreaths put there in memory of Zhou Enlai, triggering off serious rioting in the square

in 1975. The plan was for the modernisation of China's industry, farming, defence, and science. The Left put all their energy into a series of campaigns against bourgeois and outdated ideas in education and in the artistic life of China.

The Right suffered a big setback in 1976 when Zhou Enlai died. He had been a popular leader and thousands of people went to Tienanmen Square in Beijing to place wreaths there in his memory. When police removed the wreaths on 5 April, 10,000 people rioted to show their support for Zhou and for Deng Xiaoping, who now took over as Prime Minister in his place. The Left, however, cleverly blamed the riots on Deng and stripped him of all his government and Party posts. In his place they appointed Hua Guofeng, a relatively unknown politician who had risen so fast in the Party that people called him a 'helicopter'.

With Zhou and Deng out of the way, the Left, led by the Gang of Four, seemed to be in control of China's political life. And when, on 9 September 1976, the eighty-three-year-old Mao Zedong died, the Gang of Four prepared to take power. They were, however, beaten to it by the Politburo. The Politburo gave Mao's post of Party Chairman to Hua Guofeng, the new Prime Minister. As the Party Chairman also commanded the armed forces, Hua Guofeng now controlled the government, the Party and the army. Even Mao had never held such power.

With Hua in control, the Gang of Four was arrested and imprisoned within a month of Mao's death. Their arrest was followed by yet another major political campaign. In the press, on the radio and in wall posters, the Gang of Four was criticised and attacked. Jiang Qing was portrayed as a cruel, scheming, luxury-loving pornographer. Posters demanded such punishments as 'Cut Jiang Qing in Ten Thousand Pieces' and 'Deep-Fry the Gang of Four in Oil!'

Hua versus the moderates

The big question still to be answered after the arrest of the Gang of Four was which road should China follow now? Hua Guofeng and his supporters were in no doubt: they should follow in the footsteps of Mao Zedong. In 1977 they declared that whatever Mao had said must be obeyed and whatever decisions Mao had made must be put into action. Hua and his supporters were called **'Whateverists'** because of this.

The other road, of course, was the moderate one. Unfortunately for them, the moderates had no leaders in the Party at the time of Mao's death, for Deng Xiaoping had been expelled after the Tienanmen Square riot. But soon, wall posters began to appear saying such things as 'Bring Back Deng'. It appeared that public opinion was coming to favour the moderate right.

Work section

Using the information you have read in this chapter, match the statements in column A with the names in column B of the people most likely to have made them.

A1 'You want to get rid of me before my husband's body is even cold. Is this the way to show gratitude to Chairman Mao who promoted you?'

A2 'One should not talk of class struggle every day. In real life, not everything is class struggle.'

A3 'We must put all our efforts into modernising our factories, our farms, our armed forces and our technology.'

A4 'B. 52 hasn't much longer to live. He doesn't trust us. We had better act boldly. Of course, I do not deny his historic role in unifying China. Now, however, he abuses the trust the people have given him. He cares only about his own power.'

B1 Jiang Qing
B2 Deng Xiaoping
B3 Zhou Enlai
B4 Mao Zedong
B5 Hua Guofeng
B6 Lin Biao

THE 'NEW HISTORICAL PERIOD': 1976 TO THE PRESENT

Between 1976 and 1980 the moderates in the Communist Party slowly gained an advantage over the more extreme 'Whateverists'. Deng Xiaoping returned to power in 1977 as deputy Chairman of the Party and as Deputy Prime Minister. Although he ranked second to Hua Guofeng in these positions, he quickly gained great influence amongst the other Party leaders.

Under Deng's influence, China entered what the Party called a '**new historical period**'. This meant that the period of upheavals under Mao Zedong was over, and that China would now follow more moderate policies. Above all, China would now put every effort into economic growth based on the Four Modernisations begun by Zhou Enlai.

Democracy Wall

An important sign that a 'new historical period' had begun appeared in 1978. A group of young people put up a poster on a wall in Beijing which said:

A. Mao Zedong was seventy per cent good and thirty per cent bad.'

A month later, another poster went up with the title 'Democracy, the fifth modernisation'. It said:

B. 'Without democracy, the fifth modernisation, the other four modernisations are only a lie.'

For the whole of the next year, 1979, thousands of posters criticising Mao Zedong were pasted to a wall in Changan Avenue, the main street in Beijing. Printed on brightly coloured paper, the posters attracted large crowds. Unofficial papers and journals criticising Mao were openly sold and read. People got up on soap boxes and made speeches, demanding

Democracy Wall in Beijing, 1979

greater freedom. As a result, this stretch of wall became known as **Democracy Wall**.

This new period of free speech made Deng Xiaoping and the moderates even more popular. By 1980 Deng was popular and powerful enough to demote Hua Guofeng and the 'whateverists' to less important posts, replacing them with moderate supporters of his own. The most important of these were Zhao Ziyang, who became Prime Minister in 1980, and Hu Yaobang who became Party Chairman in 1981.

No sooner had the moderates gained control of the Party than they clamped down on free speech. Wall-posters were banned, Democracy Wall was closed to the public in 1979, and the leading poster writers were arrested.

The trial of the Gang of Four

Then, in the winter of 1980–1, the Gang of Four were put on trial. They had been in prison since their arrest in 1976. Once the trial began, it soon became clear that it was not only the Gang of Four who were being judged. The record of Mao himself was also on trial. The Chief Prosecutor summed up the charge against Mao when he said:

C. 'The people are very clear that Chairman Mao was responsible, so far as his leadership was concerned, for their plight during the Cultural Revolution . . . However, they will never forget or obliterate his great contributions to . . . founding the People's Republic of China and pioneering the socialist cause in China. Chairman Mao's great achievements are primary, while his mistakes are secondary.'

All of the Gang of Four were found guilty and sentenced to long terms of imprisonment.

By 1982, the left wing of the Communist Party – the Gang of Four, the 'Whateverists' and all other kinds of Maoists – had been discredited. Under Deng Xiaoping's moderate influence, the government was able to concentrate on China's pressing economic and social problems.

The need for modernisation

The greatest problem facing the government in the 1980s was the same as that in 1900: the grinding poverty in which most Chinese people lived. Their poverty was made worse by serious droughts and floods in two provinces in 1980–1.

The way to attack poverty was to increase the output of both industry and agriculture. In 1979 a new and ambitious Ten-Year Plan was introduced. Many new factories were built. Workers were paid bonuses for extra output. People were allowed to start their own small businesses. More consumer goods, such as clothes, bicycles and cosmetics were made.

In the countryside the size of peasants' private plots was increased. A **Responsibility System** for commune land was started in 1978, by which families were given responsibility for cultivating areas of land within their commune. They signed contracts promising to produce fixed amounts of food for sale to the state, and were allowed to sell any surplus at market for their own profit.

'The enemy in the womb'

Perhaps the most difficult economic problem facing China in the mid-1980s concerned the amazing growth of the Chinese population.

In 1982 a census of the population showed that 1,015,410,000 people lived in China, three quarters of them working in agriculture. At a low estimate, this massive population was increasing by roughly twelve million each year. Chinese planners worked out what would happen over the next hundred years if the population continued to grow at that rate. The planners' forecasts are shown in this graph:

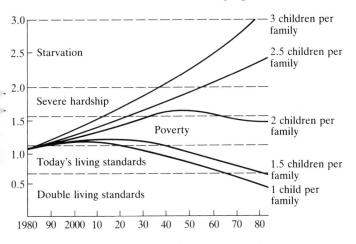

Putting it another way, if every Chinese couple between 1980 and 2000 had three children, all their grandchildren would live either in poverty or in severe hardship; while all their great grandchildren would face either severe hardship or starvation. And at the time when the planners did their calculations, Chinese women were bearing an average of three children each in the course of their lives. In 1981 nearly two million babies were born into families that already had at least five children.

To fight what the planners called 'the enemy in the womb', the government began a **One Child Policy** in 1980. This was a series of measures to discourage couples from having more than one child. To discourage couples from having children when young, the minimum age for marriage was set at 20 for women and 22 for men. Couples wanting to marry had to get the consent of their commune and take a written test in family planning. To discourage couples from having more than one child, those with one child only were given generous family allowances and more ration coupons. Single children found it easier to get into higher education, while their parents got housing priority and larger plots of land. For people willing to be sterilised there were also extra holidays and cash payments.

By the mid-1980s the One Child Policy had already started to succeed in the cities. But in the countryside it did not always work as intended. In remote areas where Party workers had less influence than in the cities, some couples simply ignored the policy. So in the rich southern province of Guangdong, for example, the rate of population growth actually rose in the 1980s.

Another unintended result of the One Child Policy came from the fact that the Chinese traditionally value sons more than daughters; thousands of baby girls were therefore murdered after birth so that the parents could try again for a son without going against the policy.

Work section

A. Study sources A-C in this chapter, then answer these questions:
1. In source C, suggest what the Chief Prosecutor meant by the 'plight' of the people.
2. In what way does source A agree with source C?
3. How does source C suggest that the plight of the people was Mao's responsibility?

B. Study the graph above, then answer these questions:
1. According to the graph, how many people would starve by the year 2080 if every couple in the 1980s had three children?
2. According to the graph, can the population growth problem be solved by limiting families to two children? Explain your answer.
3. Does the graph suggest that the One Child Policy is the only possible solution to the problem of population growth? Explain your answer.

C. List the methods used by the government to discourage couples from having more than one child, then answer these questions:
1. What criticisms can be made of these methods? How might a Party official defend them?
2. Do you think that the advantages of the One Child Policy are greater than or less than the disadvantages? Explain your answer.

20

CHINA AND THE WORLD, 1949 TO THE PRESENT

The Communists came to power in China shortly after the start of the 'Cold War' between the USA and the USSR. An atmosphere of mutual fear and suspicion had led to a complete breakdown in relations between the two countries.

As the USSR was a Communist country, it was natural that the new Chinese government should want to be its friend and ally. However, the Treaty of Friendship, Alliance and Mutual Assistance which they signed in 1950 (see page 32) alarmed the United States government. The Americans feared that Communism would now spread from the USSR and China into other countries, especially in South-East Asia.

Two events in 1950 seemed to confirm the Americans' suspicions. First, in October, Chinese forces invaded Tibet, overthrowing its ruler, the Dalai Lama, and making the country into part of the People's Republic of China. Second, when a war began in Korea between the Communist north and the American-backed anti-Communist south, China sent 300,000 troops to help North Korea. For the next three years, 1950 to 1953, Chinese and North Koreans fought an expensive and bloody war against South Koreans and an American army, officially called a United Nations force because it also contained units from Britain and other United Nations countries.

As a result of fighting against United Nations troops, the People's Republic of China was not allowed to join the United Nations Organisation. Instead, Chiang Kaishek's government on the island of Taiwan was recognised as the true government of China, and was given a place in the UNO. The Korean War also made the Americans decide to support Chiang Kaishek. From 1954 onwards the American navy protected Taiwan from possible Communist attack by patrolling the Taiwan Straits.

The Sino-Soviet split

The hostility of the UNO and of the American government to Communism made the relationship between China and the USSR much stronger. In 1956, however, their relationship started to cool. A new Soviet leader, Nikita Khrushchev, began to develop more friendly relations with the USA and other capitalist countries in the West. The Chinese strongly disagreed with his view that there could be a state of 'peaceful co-existence' between Communist and capitalist countries. This disagreement was made worse by a series of armed clashes between Soviet and Chinese troops along the Amur River, the border between the two countries.

The Sino-Soviet split, as this disagreement between China and the USSR was known, became so deep that the Soviets stopped all economic aid to China by 1960. In 1964 tension increased when China tested its own atomic bomb. Further armed clashes on the Ussuri River in 1969, and in other border areas in 1974 and 1978, led many people in both countries to predict a major war between them in the foreseeable future.

China and the USA

China's relations with the USA remained bad throughout the 1960s. In addition to the American presence in Taiwan, China was alarmed by the USA's role in the Vietnam War.

From the early 1960s onwards, the United States sent troops and supplies to help the anti-Communist South Vietnamese fight Communist North Vietnam and Communist Vietcong guerillas. With American bombers dropping bombs only miles from the border between China and Vietnam, relations with the USA were bound to be poor.

In the late 1960s the Americans began to withdraw their army from Vietnam. In 1971 talks between the American and Chinese governments led to a big improvement in their relations. Even more promising, in 1971 the United Nations accepted the People's Republic as a member and expelled Taiwan from its Security Council. Following a visit to Beijing by President Nixon in 1972, trade and cultural links were established. In 1979 the USA gave full diplomatic recognition to the People's Republic, and a visit to Washington by Deng Xiaoping cemented the new agreement.

China's southern neighbours

As you have read, Chinese forces invaded and occupied Tibet in 1950. In 1959 the Tibetans rebelled against Chinese rule. After heavy fighting Chinese troops crushed the rebellion and forced the Dalai Lama to flee to India. Over the next few years around 9000 Tibetans followed the Dalai Lama into exile, leaving their country to be run as a Chinese province until 1965 when it became an autonomous region within the People's Republic, theoretically running its own affairs.

The Tibetan issue led to a conflict between China and another of her southern neighbours, India. The Indian government was friendly towards China for much of the 1950s, but the events in Tibet made the Indians fear China's intentions. In 1962 fighting

A Chinese Communist leader reads a proclamation from Beijing to a crowd of Tibetans in Lhasa, the capital of Tibet, shortly after the Chinese army crushed the Tibetan rebellion in 1959

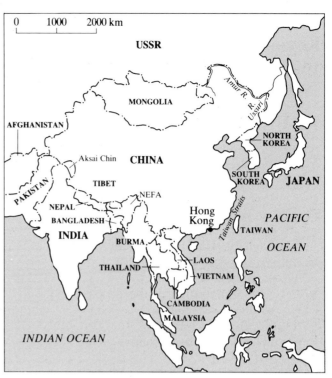

China and her neighbours

broke out along their eastern and western borders after a dispute over the ownership of the North-East Frontier Agency (NEFA) and Aksai Chin. The Chinese easily beat the Indian forces, and although they withdrew from the NEFA, they have remained in Aksai Chin ever since.

From 1962 to 1979 China was at peace with its southern neighbours. But in 1979 a dispute with Vietnam, now united under Communist rule, turned into full-scale war. A year earlier the Vietnamese government had signed a treaty with the USSR, China's bitter enemy. When the Vietnamese increased their influence in South-East Asia by marching into Laos and Kampuchea, China invaded Vietnam at the start of 1979. The aim was to stop this ally of the USSR from gaining power to the south of China. After inflicting considerable damage on Vietnam, the Chinese withdrew in March 1979.

China and the world in the 1980s

Throughout the 1980s, China steadily increased her contacts with the rest of the world. As part of the Four Modernisations programme, China bought increasing amounts of military and industrial equipment from abroad. Foreign tourists found it easier to visit China, while increasing numbers of young Chinese were sent abroad for higher education.

By the mid-1980s some sources of friction between China and the rest of the world had been removed. In 1984, for example, the British government agreed that Hong Kong, which Britain leased from China, was Chinese territory and that it would become part of the People's Republic when the lease ran out in 1997. And in 1986 there were even signs that the bitter and long-running dispute with the USSR was becoming less tense: a speech by the new Russian leader, Mikhail Gorbachev, suggested that the USSR was now prepared to consider the normalisation of relations between them.

Work section

A. Make a timeline showing all the events mentioned in this chapter, in the order in which they happened. You should be able to find seventeen events.

Example: 1949
1950   Treaty of Friendship between the USSR and China. China invades Tibet.
1951
1952
1953

(Use a line 19 centimetres long, with half a centimetre for each year.)

B. Make revision notes on what you have read about China under Communist rule in chapters 12–20. There is a revision guide on the next page to help you organise your notes if you need it.

Revision guide

These note-headings and sub-headings are designed to help you make notes for yourself on China under Communist rule. They are not a complete set of notes to be copied.

A. The Communist state
1. The Common Programme of the Communist Party
2. Problems facing the Communists in 1949
3. The government of Communist China

B. Years of great change, 1950–3
1. The rights of women
2. The Agrarian Reform Law, 1950
3. Problems arising from the Law
4. Economic reforms
5. The organisation of the people
   a) Party campaigns
   b) Thought reform
   c) Party interest groups

C. The first Five-Year Plan, 1953–7
1. Aims of the Plan
2. Achievements of the Plan

D. The cooperative farms
1. Mutual-aid teams
2. Lower-stage cooperatives
3. Higher-stage cooperatives

E. The Hundred Flowers episode, 1956–7

F. The Great Leap Forward, 1958
1. The communes
   a) The purpose of the communes
   b) The functions of the communes
2. Aims of the second Five-Year Plan
3. Propaganda and public enthusiasm
4. The backyard steel campaign

G. The crisis of 1959–61
1. Strains created by the Great Leap Forward
2. The failure of the backyard steel campaign
3. The farming crisis
4. Mao Zedong's responsibility and his resignation as Head of State

H. The Cultural Revolution, 1966–9
1. Arguments in the Party, 1962–6
2. Lin Biao and the PLA
3. The Little Red Book
4. The Red Guards
5. The breakdown of law and order
6. The cult of Mao Zedong
7. The end of the Cultural Revolution

I. Power struggles, 1969–76
1. Lin Biao and 'Project 571'
2. The split between Right and Left
3. The rise of the Gang of Four
4. Zhou Enlai's death and the Tienanmen Square riots, 1976
5. The rise of Hua Guofeng and the death of Mao Zedong
6. The arrest of the Gang of Four
7. The 'Whateverists' and the moderates

J. The 'new historical period' since 1976
1. The rise of Deng Xiaoping
2. Democracy Wall, 1978–9
3. The trial of the Gang of Four
4. Economic reforms since 1976
5. The problem of population growth

K. China and the world since 1949
1. The Treaty of Friendship, Alliance and Mutual Assistance, 1950
2. The invasion of Tibet, 1950
3. The Korean War, 1950–3
4. The Sino-Soviet Split
5. China's relations with the USA
6. The Tibetan rebellion, 1959
7. The war with India, 1962
8. The invasion of Vietnam, 1979
9. The easing of relations with the world in the 1980s

Chinese names

All the names in this book have been spelt using the modern Pinyin system of spelling Chinese names. The following list shows in brackets the old spelling used in most books until a few years ago, as well as how the names are pronounced.

Chiang Kaishek (Chiang Kai-shek) Cheeang Keyeshek
Cixi (Tsu Hsi) Tsoo Hsee
Deng Xiaoping (Teng Hsiao-p'ing) Dung Shyao-peeng
Feng Yuxiang (Feng Yu-hsiang) Fung Yoosheeang
Guangxu (Kuang-hsi) Gwarng-shee
Hu Yaobang (Hu Yao-pang) Hooyowbang
Hua Guofeng (Hua Kuo-feng) Hwar Gwofung
Jiang Qing (Chiang Ch'ing) Jyahng Cheeng
Lin Biao (Lin Piao) Lin Beeow
Liu Shaoqi (Liu Shao-ch'i) Leeoo Showchee
Mao Zedong (Mao Tse-tung) Mao Dzuh-dong
Puyi (Pu'yi) Pooyee
Qing (Ch'ing) Cheeng
Sun Chuanfang (Sun Ch'uan-fang) Sun Chooan-fang
Sun Yatsen (Sun Yat-sen) Sun Yatsen
Tang Jiyao (Tang Chi-Yao) Tang Jeeyow
Wu Peifu (Wu P'ei-fu) Woo Payfoo
Yan Xishan (Yen Hsi-shan) Yan Sheesharn
Yuan Shikai (Yuan Shih-kai) Yooan Sheekeye

Zhang Xueliang (Chang Hsueh-liang) Jang Shway-leeang
Zhang Zuolin (Chang Tso-lin) Jang dsowlin
Zhao Ziyang (Chao Tzu-yang) Jao Dzih-yang
Zhou Enlai (Chou En-lai) Joe En-lie
Zhu De (Chu Teh) Jew Duh
Beijing (Peking) Bay-jeeng
Chongqing (Chunking) Jong-ching
Dazhai (Tachai) Daj-eye
Guangdong (Kwangtung) Guahng-dong
Guangzhou (Canton) Guahng-joe
Huangpu (Whampoa) Huang-poo
Jiangxi (Kiangsi) Jyahng-she
Manzhouguo (Manchukuo) Manzooguo
Nanjing (Nanking) Nan-jing
Shaanxi (Shensi) Shahn-shee
Shenyang (Mukden) Shen-yang
Sichuan (Szechuan) Sij-wan
Yanan (Yenan) Yenan
Xian (Sian) She-an
Xinjiang (Sinkiang) Shin-jeeang

Quiz answers

Score one point for each correct answer. The average score for fifteen- or sixteen-year-old readers is seven.

1 Much bigger. (China, with 9,560,985 square kilometres is nearly twice the size of Europe's 4,929,000 square kilometres.)
2 Beijing.
3 False. About 38 million Chinese belong to the Communist Party out of a population of over 1000 million. So about 1 in 30 Chinese are Communists.
4 True. English comes second.
5 True.
6 False. This was true until 1956, but today Chinese books are printed to read in the same way as books in English.
7 Yuan.
8 Yangzi and Yellow.
9 True.
10 False. Industrial workers, for example, have eight wage grades ranging from 35 Yuan to 105 Yuan.

11 Soup. (Tea, which Westerners often think is the most common drink, is too expensive for many Chinese.)
12 Buddhism. It is estimated that there are 100 million Buddhists, 20 million Muslims, 3 million Catholics and 2 million Protestants in China.
13 True. There is one car to every 10,000 people. In Britain, by comparison, there is one car to every three people.
14 True. The army totals 4.7 million men.
15 Noodles and rice.
16 False. This is, however, true of Japan.
17 Hand-shaking and clapping. The Chinese never kiss in public.
18 The computer.
19 Tea.
20 True. The world's population in 1985 was 4,820,000,000. The population of China was 1,040,600,000.

Modern China